BLACK
SEA

Danube

Bosphorus

Constantinople

ADRIATIC

SEA

ITALY

GREECE

TURKEY

Gaeta

Naples

AEGEAN *Lesbos*

CORFU *Preveza*

SEA

LEVKAS

EUBOEA

Lipari Is

Messina

Gulf of Patras

Reggio ~ IONIAN

SEA

Candia

MALTA

CRETE

8

ERNLE BRADFORD

THE SULTAN'S ADMIRAL

THE LIFE OF BARBAROSSA

Book of the Month Club

This edition published in 1969 by arrangement with Hodder & Stoughton Ltd., by The Book of the Month Club Ltd., 4 Fitzroy Square, London, W.1.

C 6116951 X

Printed in Great Britain by
Lowe & Brydone (Printers) Ltd., London

FOR PHIL L. HYNES

For much good talk about this ancient sea

Lui voyait la terre, la terre entière avec ses continents, ses mers, ses côtes et ses vastes étendues désertiques, et rêvait d'un empire merveilleux qui, de l'Orient s' étendrait jusqu' au Couchant, là-bas, derrière l'oceán, dans le Nouveau Monde. Le Nouveau Monde, il rêvait de le peupler d'hommes robustes et d'y porter son étendard et sa religion. Il rêvait de conquérir les Indes et d'atteindre la Chine . . .

—Ekrem Rechid, *Barberousse*

PREFACE

No one can live for any length of time in the Mediterranean without coming across references to Barbarossa. It is true that these are usually no more than scraps of local folklore: Barbarossa's Cave "where he kept some of his ravished maidens," Barbarossa's Lookout "where he spied for passing ships to loot," and so on. During my years in Malta, Sicily, and elsewhere, I had met many such epithets applied to local places, and had heard, or read in old-fashioned romances, tales about his cruelty, rapacity, and invincible hatred of all Christians. I had thus unconsciously absorbed the traditional European attitude towards him: he was a pirate, a murderous Barbary corsair, a footnote in history, and no more. I did not even know that there had been two Barbarossa brothers; nor that the one who had become a legend in this sea was the younger, and that it was his brother Aruj who had had the red beard which had been commemorated in the nickname.

I first began to acquire some idea of Barbarossa's true stature several years ago, when researching the siege of Malta by the Ottoman fleet and army in 1565. One of the principal leaders of the invasion force was the famous Dragut, who had largely learned his trade as seaman and soldier under Barbarossa. One authority I read described Dragut as "almost the equal of Barbarossa." Now when I considered what a distinguished man Dragut was, I grew curious to learn more about his master and mentor.

A visit to Turkey proved a revelation. Kheir-ed-Din, "Protector of the Faith" (for I now learned his Turkish name), was no pirate, but a national hero. Barbarossa was the founder of the Ottoman navy, and one of the greatest men in the history of the Turkish Empire. He was not an unlettered corsair but a man of culture, and conversant with at least six languages. He had become one of the most important figures in the court of Suleiman the Magnificent, that outstanding Sultan who was not known to tolerate the second-rate among his friends and advisers.

My revised opinion of Barbarossa was further confirmed by subsequent study in the Royal Malta Library of a number of old volumes and records relating to the origins of the Ottoman navy, the activities of the Barbary corsairs in the sixteenth century, and the history of the Kingdom of Algiers (which I now learned had been founded by the Barbarossa brothers). The picture that emerged was a fascinating one. It was also totally at variance with the malicious caricature which I, like so many others, had previously taken for a true portrait.

There can be no doubt that the two Barbarossa brothers, Aruj and Kheir-ed-Din, were men of violence—in a century that was not noted for peace in the Mediterranean area. Unlike so many *condottieri* and soldiers of fortune, however, the Barbarossas (and in particular Kheir-ed-Din, by far the greater of the two) were men of *constructive* violence. They fought their enemies and destroyed their cities and shipping in order to create a new kingdom on the North African coast. Whereas the Genoese Admiral Andrea Doria left behind him little but a name, written on the forgetful waters of the Mediterranean, Kheir-ed-Din established a kingdom, organised a fleet, and originated a dockyard system that was to serve the Ottoman Empire efficiently for many years. He changed the balance of power at sea so effectively that he was largely responsible for the massive expansion of that empire during the reign of the Sultan Suleiman.

PREFACE

I found that most of the misrepresentations of Kheir-ed-Din's character originated from France—for reasons which become apparent in the concluding chapters of this book. Contemporary chroniclers, even of his greatest adversary, Spain, were almost unanimous in according him respect, a just estimate of his achievements, and a genuine admiration.

This is not an attempt to rehabilitate Barbarossa, who does not need it, but to strip away some of the veils of varnish and inaccurate overpainting that have disguised from Europeans the portrait of a very remarkable man. He bears comparison with Sir Francis Drake in his aptitude as a sailor and a military leader, and in the pattern of his life. Both men rose from humble origins to positions of great power and influence. Both started their careers "on the wrong side of the law" (such as it was), and ended with high honours bestowed upon them by their sovereigns. Kheir-ed-Din, perhaps, had a longer-lasting effect upon history. The Kingdom of Algiers, which he founded, was largely to determine the pattern of life and trade in the Mediterranean until the early nineteenth century.

I have been fortunate enough to visit, at one time or another, almost all the places that feature in the history of Barbarossa's turbulent life throughout this sea. Many of the capes, harbours, and anchorages, from Djerba to the lonely Lipari Islands, I saw first from the decks of small vessels or sailing boats. At Djerba, indeed, where the lateen-sailed trading craft still loiter in the bright lagoon, it is not hard to "see Barbarossa plain"; nor, when the peaks of Levkas lift out of an Ionian morning mist, to relive the day when Andrea Doria fled before the Sultan's Admiral.

E. B.

1968

CONTENTS

CONTENTS

ILLUSTRATIONS

Between pages 112 and 113

MAPS

THE SULTAN'S ADMIRAL

B

1

GALLEYS OF THE RAIDERS

Majestically the great galley drove on southward bound down the coast. In the distance, out of sight below the rim of the horizon, her consort followed. To port of the leading vessel the tawny hills behind the coastal plain of western Italy burned under the summer sun. To starboard lay the rocky island of Capraia. Beyond it, the northern peninsula of Corsica reared up against the hard blue sky. The sea was calm and there was too little wind to fill the great lateen sails. So the two ships came on, "negligently rowing along, no less than ten leagues asunder, careless, indolently supine, and, according to custom, in very indifferent order . . ."

It was the year 1504 and the two galleys so innocently running down the Italian coast belonged to no less a dignitary than Pope Julius II. At that time the occupant of St. Peter's chair was not averse to a little speculation in mercantile trading, and the galleys had recently loaded at Genoa with locally manufactured goods, imported luxuries, and silks and spices from the East. They were bound for the port of Civitavecchia, a little north of Rome, to unload their goods for transport to the capital by road.

The leading galley was the papal flagship, an ornate and elaborately decorated vessel—the flower of the shipbuilder's craft. About 150 feet in length, riding the sea to the easy beat of her oars, she looked from a distance more like a work of art than a practical vessel designed for war or commerce. Her sails were brailed up along the two great curving yards that soared like wings above her fore and main masts. Except with a fair and following wind from astern, when she could run goose-winged before it, it was upon the motive power of her rowers that she mainly depended. Now, in the high Mediterranean summer, the oarsmen got little respite.

At the prow and poop a short deck provided accommodation for the fighting men and the sailors who worked the yards. They were at rest, reclining under awnings, anticipating no danger in this pacific part of the Italian seaboard. With them also there were trumpeters and heralds—those guardians of the pomp and authority so dear to the heart of Renaissance Europe. The poop itself was elaborately carved, painted, and gilded, and flaunted a purple damask awning under which the captain, chief officers, and other gentry embarked for the passage sat at their ease. On a special platform above the poop the pilot and the helmsman directed the great vessel; the one giving his orders for the course, while the other leaned as necessary against the long tiller that was attached to the centre-line rudder.

Apart from the centre-line rudder in place of the old steering oar, there was little about this galley that would have been unfamiliar to the ancient Romans or the Greeks. Perhaps a certain improvement in the sails—lateens instead of square sails—and a greater degree of colour and decoration might have been remarked. Other than that, the main distinguishing feature of the galley—the original reason for her whole existence as a fighting ship—had remained little changed throughout the centuries. The great beaked prow standing out proudly from the forward fighting platform was a direct legacy from the ram of the classsical world. Although techniques of fighting had changed with the advent of artillery—the forward guns taking over much of the old duties of the ram—it remained an integral part of the warship. The long prow could still be used to impale the ship's side of an enemy while the fighting men harassed her with arquebus fire as well as crossbow bolts and arrows, until such time as they could leap aboard and take her with cold steel.

Beautiful indeed as such a ship was, there was another side to her: something that explained the perfumes and unguents worn by the gentry on the poop, or held to their noses in delicately pierced pomanders. "It is not necessary to look far to find an extreme contrast with the pride of the galley's appearance. At the very moment that the galley dazzles one's eyes with her sculptures, her draperies and her movement through the water, she horribly affronts one's nostrils, and exudes throughout her whole length the utmost misery . . ."

Now, as the papal galley altered course slightly to pass through the five-mile-wide channel between the island of Elba and the mainland of Italy, a watcher standing on the rocky cliffs of Piombino might have thought her beautiful indeed. The very way in which, between each stroke, the blades of her oars were momentarily suspended above the water, like the wings of a hovering falcon, would have entranced the eye. Then, as they dipped again in one easy flowing motion, she glided swiftly forward. But it was the motive power for these oars, the wretched toiling men who, in their semidarkness and stench, made the galley repulsive to the nostrils. Hygiene was little comprehended in the sixteenth century, and a galley's bilges—even though regularly pumped out—were foul from men who were compelled to urinate and defecate at the very benches where they laboured in their chains.

Below decks in the long waist of the ship, seated four, five, or six at the heavy looms of the oars, the galley's "machinery" was at work. "They are chained six to a bench," one who was himself a galley slave tells us. "The benches are four feet wide covered with sacking stuffed with wool over which are thrown sheepskins which reach to the deck beneath them. The officer who is master of the galley slaves remains aft with the captain to receive his orders. There are two under officers, one amidships and one at the prow; and all of them are armed with whips, with which they flog the totally naked bodies of the slaves. When the captain gives the order to row, the officer gives the signal with a silver whistle which hangs on a cord around his neck. The signal is repeated by the under officers and very soon all the fifty oars strike the water as if one. Imagine six men chained to a bench as naked as they were born, one foot on the stretcher, the other raised and placed on the bench in front of them, holding in their hands an oar of immense weight, stretching their bodies towards the after part of the galley with arms extended to push the loom of the oar clear of the backs of those in front of them, who are in the same attitude. They plunge the blades of the oars into the water and throw themselves back, falling onto the seat which bends beneath their weight. Sometimes the galley slaves row thus ten, twelve, even twenty hours at a stretch, without the slightest respite or rest. On these occasions the officer will go round, putting into the mouths of the wretched rowers pieces of bread soaked in wine to prevent them from fainting . . ." Small wonder then that Grossino, a North Italian visitor to Rome, viewing some Turkish galley slaves, could remark: "Poor creatures! They must envy the dead."

Most of these men who drove the beautiful papal galley on her way down the coast were Moslems—either captured Turks, Arabs, or Moors from the North African coast. The complement of the oar benches was also reinforced by condemned criminals, and by a third class of galley slave, the "volunteers." The latter were men who had fallen into debt and who, to escape the harsh punishment inflicted on debtors, had preferred to serve at the oar. Their small wages were then paid directly to their creditors until such time as their debts were discharged. But increasingly throughout the sixteenth century, as the conflict between East and West in the Mediterranean reached new heights, it was the captured and enslaved enemy who formed the bulk of the crew below decks.

Viewed by a lookout above Piombino, the galley, as she neared the narrow strait, would have resembled some colourful water insect. Her great oars, the *remi di scallocio,* seemed to walk the hull on legs across the still blue water. But this galley, in any case, had long been under observation.

The island of Elba lies like a fish off Piombino, with its head pointed towards Corsica and its forked tail towards the mainland. It was important for its iron ore and for its skilled metalworkers, and there was a regular trade between Elba and the ports supplying Rome and the other inland cities of Italy. It was this, perhaps, which had lured up into a sea hitherto "safe for Christians" the lean Turkish galleot that now idled under the shadow of the great rocks, hidden in a cove below the northern fin of the island. On the other hand, it was just as likely the knowledge that the coastal route between Elba and Piombino was much followed by rich merchant ships bound for Rome which had brought so far north the sea captain Aruj and his Turkish crew.

In marked contrast to the large papal galley now entering the channel, the Moslem galley (technically a galleot because of her size) had no more than eighteen banks of oars on either side, as compared with the twenty-seven of the Christian vessel. She was a great deal shorter on the waterline as well as in beam, while her lighter oars were worked by only two or three men. In this case, however, there was a further and important difference—

7

the galleot was manned entirely by Turkish freemen. Too small to be worked on the slave system of the larger Christian vessel, her oarsmen were also fighting men. If the larger ship had the advantages of her greater strength, speed, fire power, and numerous soldiers aboard, she was not wholly manned by men eager for conflict and desperate for plunder.

Even so, as the Turks who had been watching the approach of the galley from a vantage point above the headland ran down to acquaint their captain, Aruj, there was some doubt and hesitation among the crew. Aruj himself had none, set the men to the oars, and made out into the channel to meet the papal galley head on.

"The Turks, weighing the bulk of the galley against the feebleness of their galleot, utterly condemned the madness of the proposal, and plainly told their captain that he reflected not; that the second galley might, easily enough for their destruction, come up to its consort's assistance; adding that, instead of offering to be so rash as to attack an enemy so far above their match, and who had succour of equal force within sight, they thought it their business to make off with speed, in order to escape such evident danger.

" 'God forbid,' replied the determined Corsair, 'that I should ever live to be branded with such infamy!' "

On she came, dip, sweep, pause, and dip again—the great, heavy, beautiful bird, carving her way through the sea. Meanwhile the small, but agile and bright-eyed, hawk awaited her. There was indeed, in the conflict about to take place, something reminiscent of the loosing of a hunting hawk upon a bustard in the desert. "If the attack is successful, the spectator sees a white flutter of feather and tail, a scuffle on the ground, possibly several swoops on the part of the hawk, then all is quiet as the hawk seizes his quarry by the neck. White feathers soon fly in the breeze as the hawk plucks the breast of his prey preparatory to having a bite of its flesh . . ."

8

Aruj, the rais, or captain, of the galleot, was not the man to listen to his crew's fears. Whatever his faults, he was, above all, that unusual human being, a total "man of action." He was, perhaps, to fail in his life through not listening often enough to the cool voice of reason, yet all his successes were to derive from his ability to "grasp the nettle, danger."

By now the Turkish galleot had pulled out into the middle of the narrow channel. Aruj, sensing that the only way to ensure the fidelity of one's followers is to make quite sure that they cannot become one's deserters, ordered half the crew to let slip their oars into the sea. It says much for the discipline of a Turkish crew on a private enterprise (not backed with the authority of their own or any state), that the men did as they were told. It says much also for the authority wielded by their captain.

To let slip half their oars meant that the galleot had no chance of making her escape if things went wrong. The men aboard her were now totally committed to the battle that lay ahead. They could not for a moment have the comforting knowledge that, if they were being worsted, they could escape over the horizon, or round the rocky coast of Elba.

Fingering the red beard that was later to become synonymous with his fame throughout Europe, Aruj stood watching the great Christian ship as she approached him, all in ignorance that there was an enemy in this part of the Catholic Sea. So the great galley approached, "not imagining the galleot to be Turkish (a sight till then unknown in those seas, the Barbary cruisers being only brigantines and small rowboats), and tho' curious to know why it lay waiting, yet far from dreaming of an enemy. But being arrived near enough to take a full view of the make of the vessel, and to distinguish the Turkish habits, in the utmost hurry and consternation they began to make ready for an encounter . . ."

Now there was an immediate call to arms, and drums began to beat. The under officer lifted the silver whistle from the cord around his neck and blew the call to increase the stroke as the

9

soldiers ran for their weapons. Too late! The Turks were upon them. Aruj and his men had been poised with their muskets and their bows in their hands, and now they opened fire upon a confused and unready enemy. A second later, the beaklike prow of the galley swept alongside the papal vessel and Aruj at the head of his men leapt on board. The Turks who had been manning the oars jumped from the rowing benches, seized their weapons, and followed their leader.

Within a matter of minutes the astounded officers upon the poop, the demoralised soldiers, and the whole crew of the great galley found themselves overwhelmed. There was no option but to surrender, and the captain formally handed his sword to Rais Aruj. He, his officers and men were bound and locked below hatches. From the slaves at the oars there came great cries of joy and wolflike howlings, as all of them began to rattle their chains, to call attention to the fact that they expected their new master to free them. But Aruj had no time to waste. He called his lieutenants round him on the poop. They gathered exultantly about him, but his next words were enough to reduce even their high spirits to an uneasy silence.

"I must—and will—have the other galley! We have captured this one. Now let us capture the second!"

They argued against it. He pointed out that if the first, and largest, vessel had succumbed so easily, so would the second. Finally the man's dominant personality, combined with their recent triumph, allayed their fears. After all, had not their rais just proved himself correct against the judgement of those who had said that this vast galley was too much for them? And this time Aruj was also adding dissimulation as an additional weapon to the Turkish armoury. He ordered his captives to be stripped of their clothes and armour, and his own crew to remove their Turkish clothing and don that of the Christians. At the same time he had his galleot towed round and secured astern of the papal vessel. Now, to all intents and purposes, it would look to the second Christian ship as if the papal galley had encountered a corsair off the coast of Elba, had captured her, and was towing her off as a prize. The Turks were ever warriors, and now they were seized by Aruj's enthusiasm and lust for battle.

That hour, O Master, shall be bright for thee:
Thy merchants chase the morning down the sea,
The braves who fight thy war unsheathe the sabre . . .

Everything was ready. A Turkish overseer strode the long catwalk between the oar benches and gave the order for the stroke. The blades on the port side were poised motionless above the sea, while the men on the starboard side threw their weight into the great looms of their oars. Slowly the galley circled to port, turning her beaked prow towards her approaching companion. The whistle blew again, and one of the Turks picked up the stick alongside a tambour and prepared to give the stroke. Thrum! Both banks of oars went into action, and the oar blades struck the water in unison. "The stratagem failed not of its desired effect . . ." The other galley, seeing the leader turn towards them towing behind her a foreign galleot, immediately altered course to find out what had happened. They saw the helmeted officers on the poop, and saw too the captain pacing up and down. But they were still too far away to descry that this burly red-bearded captain was not the same as the elegant Genoese who had stood there only half an hour before.

As the two galleys closed on one another in the narrow strait between Elba and Piombino, the Turks kneeling behind the bulwarks had their arquebuses and their composite Scythian-style bows at the ready. Baba (Father) Aruj would tell them when to reveal themselves and open fire. The moment came. The kneeling Turks arose—and suddenly the unsuspecting second galley was hit by a devastating hail of arrows and lead shot. The surprise was complete. Before the officers, let alone the sailors and soldiers of the galley, had had time to collect themselves—to wonder even whether their compatriots had gone mad—the *rambade* or forward fighting prow of the other galley was alongside them, tearing through the oars on their starboard side. With a great cry of "Allah! Allaaah!" the Turks swarmed aboard their astounded opponent.

A number of the Italians on the upper deck were killed or wounded in that first fusillade, and after that "the galley was instantly boarded and carried, with very little further bloodshed or resistance." The triumphant Aruj found himself in possession of two of the largest vessels in the Mediterranean.

After disarming the officers and soldiers, his first thought was to release the Moslem rowers at the oars of both his new-found vessels. The Christian criminals or debtors could stay in their shackles to toil, but true sons of the Prophet (some of them Turks and others from the African territories) were immediately freed. Aruj and his lieutenants had a quick inspection of their Christian captives, picking out with a practised eye those who looked as if they could stand the rigours of the oar. The others would still fetch money in the slave market back home in North Africa. Those who had rich or influential relatives—whether they had been condemned to the oar or not—would one day be able to ransom themselves at a handsome profit to their captors.

Towing their own galleot behind the papal galley, the Turks turned to the south. They made their way between the rocky islands of Montecristo and Giglio. The days of hot summer passed as they crept down the Tyrrhenian Sea, then altered course to slide between Sicily and the southern tip of Sardinia towards their home port of Tunis. Sometimes a cool and favourable northerly breeze wafted from astern, and they goosewinged their great twin lateen sails. Only then was the monotonous clank of the toiling slaves (as they worked, their leg irons rattled in unison) completely stilled. Mostly though, since it was still the high heat of the windless Mediterranean summer, the two great galleys resounded day and night to the leathern voice of the tambour, the pipe of the silver whistle, and the dip, sigh, pause, and splash of the sweeping oars.

Many centuries before, the Romans had defeated their Semitic rivals the Carthaginians and had established sway over this sea. Now, with the aid of an Asiatic race, the Turks, the people from North Africa were about to reap their revenge upon the descendants of the ancient Romans. The salt-sown ruins of Carthage, the islands, the cities, seaports, and trading posts of the ancient Phoenicians—slumbering under the drunken summer sun—must have raised a ghostly cheer.

So they came swanning down the soft sea to the city that was described by an Arab chronicler as "Tunis—the White, the Odoriferous, the Flowery Bride of the West." (There were some unkind enough to say that the adjective "odoriferous" was not complimentary, but referred to the stinking salt pans and the oozy sewage-laden lagoons around the city.) The land horns of the Gulf of Tunis closed around the two captured ships and the towed galleot. Soon they saw ahead of them, rising out of the heat haze and the low-lying coastal belt, the white houses of the port that they had made their temporary home.

"The wonder and astonishment," says the sixteenth-century Spanish historian Diego Haedo, "that this notable exploit caused in Tunis, and even in Christendom, is not to be expressed, nor how celebrated the name of Aruj Rais was become from that very moment; he being held and accounted, by all the world, as a most valiant and enterprising commander. And by reason his beard was extremely red, or carroty, from thenceforwards he was generally called Barbarossa, which in Italian signifies Red-Beard."

13

2

THE BARBAROSSA BROTHERS

The island of Lesbos hangs like a pendant on the ear of western Turkey. Rich and fertile, its capital, Mitylene, fronting the continent of Asia across a ten-mile-wide channel, it had been famous in antiquity as the home of the poetess Sappho. Lesbos had also long been renowned for the excellence of its wine and its olives. Around the great Gulf of Kalloni in the west stretch the fertile plains where the vines abound and where the olives ripple like a silver sea when the north wind spins their leaves. Behind the town of Mitylene itself, another large inlet makes an excellent port, safe from the gale-force meltemi winds of midsummer.

Throughout the Middle Ages Lesbos had remained a prosperous island, secure under the protection of the Byzantine Empire. But after the sack of Constantinople by the Venetians and soldiers of the Fourth Crusade in 1204, it had suffered a similar fate to all the other Aegean Islands. It had become a trading centre dominated, as well as disputed over, by Venetian and Genoese. It was inevitable, with the decline of Christian power —Europe itself being divided into a number of warring states— that an island like Lesbos should attract the attention of the Turkish master of the Asian coast.

After his capture of Constantinople in 1453, the triumphant Sultan Mehmet II began to occupy the islands of the Aegean. As the master of Constantinople, as well as of the mainland of Greece, he could hardly tolerate these Italian enclaves in what had now become a Turkish sea. Furthermore, the possession of Constantinople had at last given the Sultan a great seaport. For the first time in their history the Turks, a predominantly land people, were faced with the necessity of creating a merchant navy, and a fighting navy to protect it. It was this, above all, which provided the main driving force behind their extraordinary naval expansion during the following century.

As for the islands, it was not only that the Sultan desired their revenues (and to be quit of Christians trading in his waters), but they had also become wasp nests of pirates. Mitylene itself was one of the most notorious havens for Catalan, Italian, and Sicilian pirates, who raided the other islands and swarmed around the mouth of the Dardanelles, preying on Turkish shipping. They even had the insolence to raid the mainland of the Sultan's dominions and carry off Turkish citizens for sale as slaves in the marts of Venice and Genoa. A Sultan who was described as "Master of the East and West, the Possessor of Men's necks, and the Peacock of the World" was not likely to tolerate such activities for long. With the aid of his recently formed navy he began systematically occupying the islands. Little did the European pirates who had operated from them realize that they had "sown the wind and would reap the whirlwind." As the Turks gradually spread into the Mediterranean world they were to produce a race of men that would make the activities of the Italian pirates in the Aegean look like children's games. Among the islands of the Aegean the Turks would learn—as had the ancient Greeks many centuries before them—the arts of navigation and seamanship. Thence they would expand throughout the whole Mediterranean, until there would not be a European sea-

port safe from them. They would go so far as to threaten great
inland cities, so that even the Pope in Rome could not be sure
that he would not wake one morning to find that his capital had
been invaded overnight by marauding Turks.

It was in Lesbos that Barbarossa and his brothers were born.
The island had fallen to the Turks in 1462 and, in accordance
with his policy of settling deserving soldiers in newly conquered
territory upon their retirement, the Sultan handed over lands and
property to the men who had helped capture the island. Among
those left behind to inherit the rich earth and the commerce that
had formerly belonged to Genoese and Venetians was the father
of the Barbarossas. He has been variously described as a "retired janissary" and a "Sipahi soldier." Certainly, although some
Spanish writers claim that he was a native Christian, there is
little doubt that he was a Moslem. His name was Ya'Kub
(Jacob), but the most reliable sources state that he himself was
the son of a Christian. This would make perfect sense if one may
assume that he had been a janissary; for all janissaries were the
sons of Christians, forcibly abducted from their parents, converted to the Moslem faith in early childhood, and then trained
to be the most formidable warriors of the Grand Turk. Although
the janissaries, so long as they served in the army, were forbid-
den to marry, it was natural that they should do so upon retirement. Ya'Kub, accordingly, married a woman of Lesbos. She
was, it would seem, the widow of a Greek priest. (Unlike the
Church of Rome, the Orthodox Eastern Church does not forbid
marriage to its clergy.)

About the ancestry of the Barbarossas one thing is certain—
there is no evidence that they had a drop of Turkish blood in
their veins. Some Christian commentators have made great
play with the fact that the two brothers who fathered Turkish
prowess at sea were not Turks, but this is irrelevant. No one has
ever denied to the Turks their prowess in warfare, or their fanat-

16

ical courage. The sons of Ya'Kub may have been Roumeliot, Albanian, or Greek in their physical lineage, but they were certainly "Sons of the Prophet" in their faith.

It is a curious thought that, when the classical Greeks of antiquity descended upon the land that they were to make their own, they dispossessed a Mother Goddess (hitherto worshipped throughout the eastern Mediterranean) and installed, among a pantechnicon of gods and goddesses, a male god, the King of the Sky. The female mother goddess was, as it were, driven underground, until, with the increasing complexities of Christianity, she reasserted herself as the Virgin Mary. The Moslem Turks now, in their turn, removed the female from the religious calendar and brought back a conception of God not so far removed from the ancient Zeus. When nations are defeated, women submit to the new conquering males, and it is an ironical fact that the mother of the Barbarossas was the widow of an Orthodox Greek priest.

"A retired janissary, described as *un honnête Musulman*, made his home [in Lesbos], married the widow of a Greek priest, and evidently prospered as a potter, since he is said to have owned a vessel for the transportation of his wares and traded sometimes as far as Constantinople. Most of the family must still have been resident there in 1501, when Venetian and French forces tried to seize the island as a suitable base for operations against the Dardanelles, on the strength of a Genoese report that it was *moult riche, fertile et prenable . . ."*

Both Turkish and Spanish records have it that Ya'Kub was a potter: an important trade then as now; and it is more than likely that he also had some acquaintance with the sea. Indeed, in an island like Lesbos, how could a man live without being familiar with the sea? The briny wind swirled the sails of the windmills that ground the corn. It drove the coasters southwards to Chios, Samos, Andros, and all the clustering islands of the archipelago. Islanders are usually seamen, and the sons of Ya'Kub were to prove that the salt was in their blood and the high north wind in their hearts.

There were four sons and two daughters of the marriage between the ex-janissary and the widow of the Greek priest. Their mother's name was Catalina. We do not know the names of her daughters, but then, in the eastern Mediterranean, daughters are nothing to boast about. A man may proudly tell you how many sons he has, but he will omit to mention his daughters.

The sons, in the order of their seniority, were Aruj, Elias, Isaac, and Khizr (later to become the most famous man in Turkey, and indeed in the Mediterranean, under his acquired name of Kheir-ed-Din). It is possible that the two girls were brought up as Christians, under the Moslem custom which permitted the females to be raised in the religion of their mother. The four boys were, without any doubt, brought up as Moslems —and there were few Moslems more dedicated to their faith than janissaries like their father. The fact that Aruj had a red beard and Khizr a brown, or auburn, beard is an indication that they were not of Turkish blood. But, in their faith, like so many converts or sons of converts, they were more dedicated than those who had never known any other religion.

Aruj, the eldest son, seems to have started his career by working aboard his father's boat; Elias to have studied to become an imam; Isaac to have been a carpenter; and Khizr, the youngest, to have helped his father in the pottery. The sixteenth-century Spanish historian Gomara as well as Diego Haedo (another contemporary, and a priest) both refer to the family background of the brothers in admiring terms. Although these historians came from the country that suffered most from the later depredations of the "red-bearded" brothers, and both were acquainted with men who had lived and worked with them, they never at any time descend to the vulgar abuse of the Barbarossas which became current among later European chroniclers. Indeed, if one may judge from their accounts, Ya'Kub and his wife and children were a model family: no hint here at all of bad upbringing leading to violent or "disgraceful" lives. The more one investigates the background of Aruj and Khizr, the clearer it becomes that it was not so dissimilar from that of Sir Francis Drake. Raised in a poor, but religious, environment, taught a craft, and expected to fend for themselves as soon as they reached manhood, these Turks were far from coming from a bad background. They were to be libelled in later centuries, but not by their contemporaries, and, just as Sir Francis Drake was to be hailed by the English as a great admiral while abused by the Spaniards as no more than a pirate, so these sons of Ya'Kub were to suffer at the hands of many European writers.

The first authentic story we hear of the early career of Aruj concerns a disastrous encounter with a galley of the Knights of St. John. The island of Rhodes, where these Christian warriors had made their home, was still firmly in their grasp. Indeed, it was not until 1522 that the Sultan, after a lengthy and bloody siege, finally expelled the knights from Rhodes. But at the time when Aruj, in company with his brother Isaac, was captain of a small galleot operating off the Dodecanese islands, the knights were very much in command of those waters. It is not known whether Aruj was at this time attempting to trade legitimately, or whether he was already embarked on a corsair's career. But in all probability, as was quite normal at the time, he was combining legitimate trade with a little piracy on the side. As the Sultan gradually expanded his sway southward through the Aegean, independent citizens were often encouraged to harass what was left of the Italian-occupied islands. Certainly there was no discredit felt in raiding the lands and possessions of the Christian enemy.

Unfortunately for Aruj, he was destined on this occasion to

fall in with one of the galleys belonging to the redoubtable Knights of St. John. "Those who have not seen a galley at sea, especially in chasing or being chased, cannot well conceive the shock such a spectacle must give to a heart capable of the least tincture of commiseration. To behold ranks and files of half-naked, half-starved, half-tanned meagre wretches, chained to a plank, from whence they remove not for months together (commonly half a year), urged on, even beyond human strength, with cruel and repeated blows on their bare flesh, to an incessant continuation of the most violent of all exercises; and this for whole days and nights successively, which often happens in a furious chase, when one party, like vultures, is hurried on almost as eagerly after their prey, as is the weaker party hurried away in hopes of preserving life and liberty."

The lookouts aboard the great galley, *Our Lady of the Conception,* sighted the Turkish galleot as she slid out from behind a wooded point. At the very same moment Aruj, Isaac, and the rest of their crew caught sight of the cross that waved on the standard above the poop of the galley. They knew at once that this vessel belonged to the greatest enemies of the Turks, and indeed of all Moslems, the Knights of St. John—"the Chivalry of the Religion" as they were proud to call themselves. The Turks bent to the straining oars. Freemen all, they were well aware of the fate awaiting them if they fell into the hands of the knights.

Had there been any wind, it is just possible that the galleot might have escaped owing to her greater manoeuvrability, but it was a calm and empty day—the weather for which the fighting galley had been developed. As the fleeing Turks sweated and strained over their oars, the galley drew remorselessly nearer. Aruj, who in later years was often enough to enjoy the satisfaction of swooping upon a fat Christian prey, now found himself in the position of a sparrow hawk that has been unwise enough to fall foul of an eagle.

On the poop of *Our Lady of the Conception* there were gathered "the knights and gentlemen, and especially the admiral or captain, who sits at the stern under a red damask canopy embroidered with gold, surveying the crew, surrounded by the chivalry of 'The Religion,' whose white cross waves on the taffeta standard over their heads, and shines upon various pennants and burgees aloft . . ." The shrill call of the under officer's silver whistle gave the order for the rowers to increase the stroke. Plash by plash, the galley drew nearer to the Turkish galleot— until it was within reach of the forward bow chasers. The seamen on the *rambade* now held their smouldering slow matches to the fuse holes of the guns, while the arquebusiers and archers stood ready to open fire.

Escape was impossible. Aruj shouted down to his crew to prepare to surrender. But before it could be made clear to the pursuing galley that they would meet with no resistance, they had begun their initial onslaught. With the first salvo from the guns and from the soldiers on her prow, Isaac, Aruj's brother, was killed outright along with a number of other Turks. The galleot was overwhelmed and "Aruj and his little company were ironed and flung into the depths of the galley until such time as they should be wanted to take their turn at the oars. In this ignominious fashion ended his first attempt at independent piracy . . ."

Now he learned for the first time, as did innumerable other sailors in those days, what the word "failure" really meant. Whether you were a Christian or a Moslem, a man or a woman, to travel upon the Mediterranean in the fifteenth and sixteenth centuries was to hazard your life and liberty. If you were a man, you might finish on the oar bench or in the slave market. If you were a woman you would end up if you were fortunate in the harem of a rich Turk, or as an unpaid drudge in the kitchen or the fields.

Life was a cheap commodity. To survive beyond childhood and beyond puberty was an achievement in itself. After that, the strong, the cunning, and the lucky might continue to enjoy the few material and sensual comforts that divert the human animal. Isaac was eliminated from the continuous conflict of the world, but Aruj and the survivors from his crew were now to serve at the oar benches.

There is no record of how long Aruj spent as a galley slave; the only fact is that he was finally ransomed—either by his father or by the Turkish merchants who had invested in his galleot. In any event, he was to learn over a period of months, possibly a year or more, the way it was to toil at the heavy loom of an oar and to fear on your cringing shoulders the thongs of the overseer's lash. He learned how the wind cries through the leather washers that were secured to the ship's side, where the oars passed through the oarports, to prevent the seas washing in. He grew used to the diet of biscuit, bean soup, a little fresh vegetable and olive oil. The soup was only served in harbour, or when the sea was completely calm, thus permitting the charcoal-fired stove to be lit. He learned, too, that the worst enemy of the galley slave is the time of bad weather when the looms of the great oars jerk back against his chest, and when the stink of the stirred-up bilges rises like death into his nostrils. Calm weather, even though they had to row, was better for the slaves, and unless they were within sight of some quarry or objective they would work "watch-and-watch," that is to say, half the oars on each side would be unmanned (the rowers sleeping or lying idle on their benches), while the other watch rowed. Then the time would come for the change of watches and the sleepers would be roused, given a meal, and, in their turn, put to work. It was during these idle hours that the oarsmen would make small carvings in wood or bone—scrimshaw work—or intricate knots and designs in rope. These products of their leisure they were allowed to sell when in harbour, to buy themselves a few luxuries, or even to indulge in the favours of some woman—herself a slave in the slave quarters.

Aruj survived, and he was finally ransomed: that is all we know about the time that he spent aboard the great galley *Our Lady of the Conception*. Shortly afterwards, it would seem that he was given the command of another ship and "for some years he followed the trade of scouring the seas, and soon became much noted and highly esteemed for his intrepidity among his associates, and failed not of signalising himself upon all occasions." Certainly his harsh training at the oar had not made him any great lover of Christians.

It was in 1492, when Aruj was about eighteen and his youngest brother Khizr fourteen or so, that a momentous event took place in the Mediterranean world, one which was to affect the pattern of life in that sea for centuries to come. At the other end of the Mediterranean, remote from the growing power of Turkey, the Spanish people finally succeeded in expelling the Moors. As Stanley Lane-Poole commented in his history *The Barbary Corsairs*: "When the united wisdom of Ferdinand and Isabella resolved on the expatriation of the Spanish Moors, they forgot the risk of an exile's vengeance. No sooner was Granada fallen than thousands of desperate Moors left the land which for seven hundred years had been their home, and, disdaining to live under a Spanish yoke, crossed the strait to Africa, where they established themselves at various strong points, such as Shershell, Oran, and notably at Algiers, which till then had hardly been heard of. No sooner were the banished Moors fairly settled in their new seats than they did what anybody in their place would have done: they carried the war into their oppressors' country."

Prior to the fall of Granada and the expulsion of the Moors, the relationships between the states of North Africa and those of Europe had been reasonably good and well conducted. Trading treaties were signed and honoured, and both sides benefited in the useful exchange of the manufactured goods of the one area for the raw materials of the other. The religious war which had long been flaming between Christian and Moslem in the East had had little effect upon the relationships between the Moslem rulers of the African Mediterranean coastline and the rulers of Europe. But all this was to change. Two quite dissimilar factors —the expansion of Turkish power in the East, and the arrival on the shores of North Africa of a revengeful Moslem population—were to combine, and to set in train a series of events that would shake Christian Europe. The action of Ferdinand and Isabella was to have unforeseen consequences. Similarly, the fall of Constantinople to the Turks, although officially regretted by the rulers of Europe (who had, in fact, denied any help to the threatened city), was to make Turkey a maritime power that would threaten and even dominate the Mediterranean sea lanes for centuries to come.

Men of ability know by instinct how to seize the circumstances of their world and make them work for their own interests. Two of the sons of the retired Moslem soldier Ya'Kub were to prove this to the hilt. The dead Isaac was to be more than avenged. The eldest and the youngest of the brothers were to leave the comfortable shores of Lesbos and make their way westwards into that part of the Mediterranean which had hitherto been dominated by the European powers. While the third son, Elias, seems to have remained behind as a trader, Aruj and Khizr arrived on the shores of North Africa sometime between 1500 and 1504.

There are a number of different accounts as to how they acquired the two ships in which they set out for the land which was later to be called by distraught and frightened Europeans "the Barbary Coast." It matters very little at this remove of time, but the actions of the brothers during their lives still contain a meaning for all who inhabit the seaboard of the inland sea. The fortresses and watchtowers, many of which survive to fascinate modern visitors, were built to preserve the local people against

24

the activities of the Barbarossas and their successors. The hill towns, perched on their almost inaccessible peaks, were a direct result of the fact that it was no longer safe to live in the ancient seaports.

The year 1504 seems to be the nearest one can get to a date for the moment when Aruj, the red-bearded, and his brother Khizr came silently and determinedly to the ancient port of Tunis. No doubt they had touched previously at the island of Djerba, and no doubt they had surprised one or two trading vessels during their passage westwards from the Aegean Sea. Two galleots, the record says, were all that they possessed—two open rowing boats, that is to say, with about seventeen oars a side, each oar manned by two, or possibly three, Turks who had elected to come on a speculative piratical voyage. In a very similar way, some years later, Francis Drake was to adventure into the Spanish-dominated waters of the Caribbean with his crew of young Devonians. Both Drake and the Barbarossas, it would be fair to say, began their sea careers as pirates—and ended up as admirals and heroes of their respective nations.

3

THE HOME OF THE CORSAIRS

The city of Tunis, to which Aruj returned in triumph with his two captured papal galleys, was very suitable for its new role as a haven for the corsairs. La Goletta, the harbour, was more than adequate for the shallow-draft galleys; there was ample water nearby; the harbour was protected from attack by fortifications; and the Sultan of Tunis had already shown himself friendly to the Barbarossa brothers. Indeed, upon his first arrival, Aruj had paid intelligent court to this Sultan of the house of Hafs, Mouley Mohammed. Both he and his brother "were kindly received by the King, who granted them free entrance and protection in his ports, with liberty to buy whatever they wanted; in return to which favour, the corsairs agreed to give him the tithe of all their purchase or booty . . ."

Now, within a brief year of concluding this business arrangement with the brothers, the Sultan had good proof of the advantages that could accrue to him and his state. "A great procession was formed of Christian captives marching two and two. Four young Christian girls were mounted on mules, and two ladies of noble birth followed on Arab horses sumptuously caparisoned.

These unfortunates were destined for the harems of their captors. The Sultan was greatly pleased at the spectacle, and as the mournful procession defiled before him, cried out: 'See how Heaven recompenses the brave!' "

Meanwhile the galley slaves were transferred from the two ships to the bagnio or slave quarters. Until such time as they might be required again at sea, their labour would be used to restore the fortifications and improve the harbour walls and defences. Fine ships though the captured galleys were, they were larger than Aruj really needed for his future operations. Throughout his life it is noticeable that he rarely used large galleys, which required a captured slave population to row them. The large galley of those days was the battleship of a later century—and a battleship was not what the determined corsair needed for his business. To pursue the modern analogy, he needed a destroyer: a swift, easily manoeuvrable raiding vessel. The time would come when the Barbarossas were forced to keep large galleys, manned by slaves, in order to engage their enemies on equal terms. But so long as their main objective was raiding the European shipping lines, the lean galleot manned by Turkish freemen was far more to their purpose.

Aruj's brother Khizr (Kheir-ed-Din) is reputed by some authorities to have begun his service as an oarsman in Aruj's ship. Certainly, it is a fact that at the famous battle of Preveza in 1538 many of the victorious Turkish galleys under the younger Barbarossa were part-manned by Turkish freemen. These volunteers, often janissaries by origin, were regarded as more efficient (and naturally far more trustworthy) than slaves, who might be expected to mutiny at the first available opportunity. Another great advantage in employing your own race at the oar was the fact that, when battle commenced, the oarsmen themselves became part of the fighting force. In the large Christian galleys, on the other hand, the oarsmen were redundant—indeed a dangerous liability—the moment that an engagement actually started. A Turkish galleot, therefore, manned on the system adopted by the Barbarossas, might be half the size of a European galley, but every man in her would be a fighting man, and every man in her would be a Turk, or fellow Moslem, eager for battle.

Aruj's technique in these early years seems to have been to keep one large galley, manned by slaves, in company with him, while relying upon a number of galleots to do the fighting and secure the prizes. The galley was something of an "insurance policy," kept at hand in case a fighting vessel of her own size might be encountered. In our own century this method of operating against enemy shipping might be compared to having a flotilla of destroyers in company with a heavy cruiser, the latter being on call if need be, but otherwise nearly all the work being done by the destroyers.

As evidence of this we find that Aruj now "armed out both the galleots and one galley." Leaving Tunis quickly before the advent of winter closed the sea to shipping "he scoured the coasts of Sicily and Calabria, taking several vessels, and a considerable number of slaves . . ." As in the ancient world, the sailing season was extremely limited, and with the first signs of bad weather both merchantmen and warships were laid up until the spring (usually the month of May), when they were launched once again.

The astonishing success of this first year's operations out of the port of Tunis must have been more than encouraging to the brothers and the Sultan. But it could not be expected that this sudden arrival in the waters of the western Mediterranean of Turkish warships would go unnoticed in the courts of Europe. For the first time for many years the news of these shipping disasters began to suggest to the European powers that some concerted action might have to be taken. But the time was not ripe for any such combined effort. Countries and nations that were just beginning on the road towards nationalism were unlikely to be able to co-ordinate against a common enemy. The extraordinary success of the Barbarossas over the years to come was largely promoted by the fact that "a house divided against itself cannot stand." It is a lesson that, even four centuries later, has not yet been learned by the nations of Europe.

The terrain, the coastland, and the natural harbours, lakelike lagoons, salt pans, fertile strips and desert wastes that the Turkish corsairs were now to establish as their home is still little known to Europeans. Soldiers and sailors who fought in the North African campaigns of the Second World War made some slight acquaintance with this land—a land that can be as fertile and beautiful as any place on earth, but which can also show its granite teeth in hard headlands, shifting coastlines, dangerous shoals, and savage storms.

When the northerlies whirl down across the narrow strait of Sicily, any vessel caught with the lee shore of Africa under her must beware. Conversely, when the khamsin blows up hot and furious off the deserts east of Tunis and south of Malta the sailor in these narrow seas must look to his canvas—and to his life. As the *Admiralty Pilot* warns: "The wind is at first light from between east and south-east. The wind veers southward, and meanwhile a thin veil of cirrus cloud often spreads across the sky from westward . . . The southerly wind strengthens and veers, with rising temperature, falling humidity, and increasing dustiness; the wind may reach gale force from southward or south-westward, blowing in scorching gusts, with rapid oscillations of temperature and humidity . . . A few drops of rain may reach the ground in the vicinity of the front during the hot season, while in the transition seasons thunderstorms occur at times; the rain in these storms frequently carries down a considerable quantity of mud, consisting of fine dust and sand picked up by the wind over the desert."

Section of North African Coast

It is a dangerous sea at many times of the year. But, with its
many inlets and headlands, rocky bays and concealed lagoons, it
remains a fine area for the seaman who has learned his native
coast, and who is intent on robbing the rich shipping lanes. Certainly in the early sixteenth century, when the Barbarossas first
introduced Turkish sea power into this area, the shipping lanes
were rich indeed. The Western world, cut off from its ancient
trade routes with the East by the Turkish nation spread like a
scimitar across Asia, had been forced to discover the overseas
routes that could connect with the necessary raw materials, as

30

well as the luxuries, of the East. The European expansion throughout the world, and its opening up of shipping lanes to the Orient, was not prompted by an abstract love of scientific discovery. It was induced almost entirely by the sheer necessity of finding another way to recommence a trade that had been closed by Turkish and Moslem power in the East.

But now that the Spaniards had established sailing routes to the riches of the American continent—which they had, to their surprise, found barring their passage to the Far East and China —their galleons were annually returning laden with gold, uncut gem stones, and the natural wealth of a hitherto unexploited world. France, Holland, and England in the years to come were not slow to follow these pioneers of Atlantic navigation, and the trade of Europe was amazingly revivified by the return from the western side of the Atlantic of enterprising seamen, backed by enterprising investors. The Strait of Gibraltar, which in the ancient world had been regarded as the "Pillars of Hercules" (the end of any normal sailing route or trading), suddenly became the open-sesame to a world of hitherto unimaginable richness. Through the narrow gap between the great cloud-trailing rock on the European side and the rock of Ceuta in North Africa, there began to pass argosies of wealth that could hardly fail to excite the greed of the new race of corsairs—especially of the expelled Moriscos who, for so many centuries, had lived happily in Spain. The western basin of the Mediterranean, which previously had been of less importance than the eastern, took on a new lease of life. It was at this very moment in history that the expulsion of the Moslem people from Spain coincided with the ejection of the Christians from the east after the capture of Constantinople in 1453. At the same time, by a strange accident of fortune, there arrived upon the scene the extraordinary Barbarossa brothers.

The territory which these Turkish sea rovers were to make peculiarly their own ranged from Tripoli, due south of Malta, to Tangier, and beyond to some of the small Moroccan ports on the Atlantic. From these latter the Moslems were soon to harry merchantmen returning from America, before they had even entered the Mediterranean.

The coastline of North Africa is remarkable for its excellent harbours—something comparatively rare in this tideless sea—and it was this fact, above all, that gave the area its special value to the Barbarossas. Moving westward from the secure harbour of Tripoli, less than a hundred miles away lies the island of

Djerba, concealing behind its palm-fringed sandy shores a beautiful great lagoon whose only access is through one narrow channel at the western end. A whole armada of ships could lie safely at anchor here, and rest secure whatever winds splintered the dangerous Gulf of Gabès. This gulf was rendered particularly treacherous to shipping by its variable and tricky currents, and by the shifting sandbanks that fringed its shores. Two islets due north of Djerba, Chergui and Rharbi, provided a convenient resting place for the marauding galleys, and an excellent lookout post for traffic passing south of Lampedusa through the channel eastward to Malta. A little north of them on the mainland lay the ancient city of Mahdia, usually referred to by contemporary writers as Africa, since this was the name given to the cape on which it stood. The small harbour there, now silted by the sand of centuries, was more than adequate for galleys that rarely drew more than six foot of water. North again, the great arm of Cape Bon thrust itself out into the strait of Sicily—perfect vantage point from which to watch for traffic bound for the southern ports of that island. Within the next gulf lay Tunis itself, and then beyond it there were the ancient harbours of Carthage and of Porto Farina, ravaged by time and the destruction of centuries but still adequate for shallow-draughted vessels. Westwards Bizerta and Tabarka, Bône, and Djidjelli beckoned the mariner—good harbours all of them, and with rich coastal land behind and always adequate water, fed by the watershed towering above the fertile coastal strip. Still further to the west lay Bougie, Algiers, Shershell, Tenez, and Oran with its superb port of Mers-el-Kebir. Quite apart from its harbours the land grew corn, olives, dates, vines, and almost every kind of fruit. Its inhabitants were mainly Berbers with an admixture of Arabs: the mountain people hardy and warlike, and the coastal people industrious farmers. With such a springboard behind them—food to nourish and harbours to shelter—it was little wonder that the warlike Turks would soon begin to shake the trade of Christendom.

While the winter harassed the Mediterranean, and while throughout all its ports seamen and merchants withdrew into the interior world of home, market place, and tavern, Aruj and his men quietly prepared for the coming spring. They were rich now, rich in possessions such as jewels and clothing, as well as in slaves. They could afford to enjoy the pleasures of a city like Tunis, whose comparatively unsophisticated inhabitants were still unaware that, though the Turk is a Moslem, he is a very different man from his Arabic coreligionists.

When the spring came, the almond blossom to break in bloom, and the short-lived wild flowers to carpet all the Mediterranean islands, two galleots and one galley left the ancient Goletta of Tunis. They turned to the northeast and made their way towards the coast of Sicily. Aruj was well aware that, with the beginning of the sailing season, he might expect to find galleys making their way down from Italy to trade with Palermo or Messina. He passed the small sleepy Aegadian Islands lying off Trapani in western Sicily, while from the vantage point of the high peak of Marettimo the frightened islanders waited and watched to see whether these invaders of their waters would land in search of food, women, and slaves. But the galleots and the galley went on steadily to the north. In the narrow strait to the east of them lay the island of Favignana. Off here, in 241 B.C. the galleys of the newly founded Roman navy had won the First Punic War by annihilating the Carthaginian fleet. The waters off Sicily, so it was said, had run red that day, as they still do after the *mattanza* when the giant tunny are slain. Now, issuing out of the Gulf of Tunis, so close to ancient Carthage, came galleys from the east destined to take their revenge upon the west. The eternal pendulumlike swing of power in the Mediterranean basin was about to reverse itself.

The galleys altered course north of Cape San Vito and began to patrol to the eastward, hoping to catch some early merchantman laden from Italy, and eager to do business with the fruit market of Sicily at Palermo. They slid gently towards the Lipari Islands, sometimes being lucky enough to catch a favourable wind on their quarter so that they could hoist the sails and give the oarsmen some relief. The islands came up ahead of them, Alicudi, Filicudi, harsh Salina, tempestuous Vulcano, and smouldering away on the northern horizon the domed sides of Stromboli, where the lava ran down hissing into the sea. At night they saw its peak pulsating with fire. The ancients had graphically termed it "the lighthouse of the Mediterranean."

It was after several days of stormy weather from the north-west that the lurking galleots saw their prize. She was a large Spanish sailing vessel that had wallowed far to the south of her course—blown in the direction of the Liparis, when she should have been heading up for Naples and its sheltering bay. The galleots closed in on the great ship, and found to their surprise that they met with no resistance at all. So they "had the good fortune to take, without striking a stroke, a very large ship, on which were five hundred Spanish soldiers, and a great quantity of pieces of eight, sent from the Catholic king to recruit and pay his army in the Kingdom of Naples."

The reason the Turks were able to capture the ship without firing a shot was that the troops aboard were all either devastated by seasickness or worn out by working at the pumps of the leaking and waterlogged vessel. This year 1505 was indeed a bad one for King Ferdinand of Spain. It is interesting to note that this is the first occasion we hear from the Spanish chronicler Zurita of the activities of Turkish corsairs in the waters of Italy and Sicily. The previous year's attack and capture of the two papal galleys had certainly not gone unremarked in Rome and Italy, but this year's capture of the money destined to pay the garrison in Naples—as well as the troops intended to relieve some of the Spanish soldiers stationed there—was important enough to cause a considerable stir in the Spanish court. That the Turks were masters of most of the eastern Mediterranean was a fact well enough known to the European powers. But now they suddenly found that the waters of the western Mediterranean, hitherto secure for their navigation, were invaded. Small vessels adventuring off the Barbary Coast of North Africa, able to prey only upon local trading vessels, had long been an accepted hazard. But the arrival of determined Turks—Turks who seemed so quickly to have learned the arts of navigation and of sea warfare—was a bad blow to European morale. It was seen, at last, that the fall of Constantinople to the soldiers of the Sultan was not just an obscure event happening far away in the Levant, but something that would affect the fortunes of Europe for centuries to come.

Of Aruj and his subsequent triumphal return to Tunis we learn that "Returning to the Goletta, he brake up his gallies, and some other prizes, and built two stout galleots, which vessels, being light and nimble, he found more to his purpose than heavy gallies. These, with two others, he equipped out to the best advantage, and, being already possessed of many Christians, he culled such as were fitted for the oar . . ." But it is doubtful whether Aruj departed so much from his normal practice of having Turkish freemen at the oars of his galleots.

By 1510, five years after this successful exploit, Aruj was one of the richest men in the Mediterranean. He and Khizr were the masters of eight stout galleots, owners of property and slaves, and must have felt themselves kings of the Mediterranean Sea. From the horned Gulf of Tunis, through the strait of Sicily, to the far-off coasts of Calabria, Sardinia, and Corsica, their ships swept the merchantmen of France, Italy, and Spain into their bulging nets.

Tunis was not enough. The Barbarossas needed a base to themselves, where they would not be hampered by local rulers, and where they would not have to pay a tithe of their takings to a ruling Sultan. By now they knew the coastline of this part of North Africa better than any seafarers since the distant days of the Roman galley masters. They had found what seemed the ideal and perfect haven, the island of Djerba. In the year 1510 the red-bearded brothers, together with their sailors and fighting men, moved from Tunis and left behind the sheltering arms of the Goletta. They made their way southward to Djerba, famous in antiquity as the home of the lotus-eaters, but destined to become even more famous among Europeans as "the lair of the Corsairs."

4

FAILURE OF AN
EXPEDITION

For the next few years the Barbarossas were to make their home, and their main base for naval operations, in the sandy, sunburned island of Djerba. The large lagoon between the island and the mainland, Bahiret el Bu Grara, some ten miles from east to west by fifteen from north to south, was ideal for harbouring the galleys and galleots. The local Berber people were friendly, and the island, as well as the mainland behind it, was rich in fruits and corn and grapes. Not all Turks, even at this time, were strict Moslems when it came to alcohol, and the vine had been cultivated along this section of coast since the days of the Roman Empire.

The island was well protected. A fortress guarded the entrance to the lagoon from the west, and it was not long before the brothers began to improve its defences. They did this to ensure that they would run no risk of being trapped in the lagoon by a superior naval force bursting through the western entrance, the Ajim channel. A low-lying island, except in the centre where a few hillocks run up to a height of about one hundred feet, Djerba was protected on the north by off-lying banks of mud where even a mild breeze can raise heavy breaking seas, and on the northwest by further banks running out from the mainland coast. It was a tricky place for any navigator unfamiliar with the area—highly suitable, therefore, for a sea rover's hideout. Other shoals and shifting sandbanks along the coast on both sides of the island added to the hazards. Aruj and his men would soon grow familiar with all this coast. They could enter or leave as, and when, they wished, yet still retain the comfortable knowledge that few other seamen in the Mediterranean would willingly come down into this treacherous southern corner of the Gulf of Gabès.

Until 1510 the island had been held secure for Spain by a garrison in the fort commanding the entrance, but in that year "Don Garcia de Toledo, son of the Duke of Alva . . . received that notable overthrow, and lost his life in the island." Morgan maintains that the reason the Barbarossas went to Djerba was that the Sultan of Tunis was afraid the Spaniards would come back to take their revenge for their loss, and that he offered them the island, thinking that they would be well able to look after it without any cost to himself. There may be something in this argument. Djerba was a technical possession of Tunis, but like so many of the harbours and small coastal towns at that time, it was constantly changing hands between the local rulers and the Spaniards. The Spanish interest along all the North African coast was to maintain garrisons wherever possible, and to ensure Spain's right to trade and the security of her merchant shipping upon these waters which, even before the arrival of the Turks, had been subjected to the activities of local corsairs operating in small galleots.

Aruj Barbarossa was soon to remind His Most Catholic Majesty that the loss of Djerba was not just a small local disaster. From the moment of his arrival in 1510 and throughout the following year, "he continued his excursions, miserably ravaging all the Italian coasts; nor any trading vessel being able to stir out without immense peril, insomuch that all Europe began to ring of his depredations." The Spanish Kingdoms of Naples and Sicily were now exposed to the violence of the Turkish raiders, while their sea communications between Spain and Italy were daily at hazard. The appearance of Barbarossa's squadron rowing purposefully up the coast of Sicily, or gliding through the Aegadian Islands northward bound, to fall upon some unsuspecting coastal town or port, caused the working population to flee to the mountain villages inland. Not only was the Spanish trade route being disrupted, but even the agriculture and fishing were being brought to a standstill in the hot summer "months of the raiders." Meanwhile, after every successful attack upon a merchant ship or raid upon some undefended village, the slave markets of Tunis grew rich with the captured.

If Aruj had been content with remaining no more than the most successful sea captain and corsair of his day there seems small doubt that he could have stayed in Djerba for years—to die either in battle at sea or of old age in his island retreat. But he was a restless man and the long sand beaches, the softly leaning palm trees, and the great salt lagoon where his ships idled at anchor were not sufficient to contain his ambition. He wished to be a king, ruler of a real city: a city where there would be better opportunities for the exercise of power, and better facilities for shipbuilding. Djerba had disadvantages quite apart from its lack of any real township, the most important of these being the absence of any trees suitable for shipbuilding. We know that a number of Turkish galleots were built out of the wood from captured prizes, but this was an unsatisfactory method, and one that could hardly be relied upon, particularly as the fleet needed to expand.

By 1512, Aruj and Khizr commanded between them twelve large galleots, eight of which belonged to the two brothers, and the other four to Turkish sea captains who had heard of the choice pickings in the central Mediterranean and had sailed down from the Aegean to put themselves under the Barbarossas' command. Just as Drake, after his first successes in the Caribbean, was never to lack for volunteers to sail under his flag, so these great Turkish captains were never at a loss for ambitious, tough seamen, eager for plunder at the expense of the Christian enemy.

In the spring of 1512, just as the ships were being given their finishing touches before being launched for the cruising season, there arrived in Djerba an emissary from the former Moslem ruler of Bougie. He had been driven from his city by the Spaniards three years before, and had subsequently been forced to live in exile in the mountainous interior. The Spaniards had planted a garrison in Bougie which commanded both the town and the port. The message delivered to Aruj was simple and to the point: "If he was prepared to invest the town from the sea, the exiled king would come down from the mountains with his Zouave troops and engage the Spaniards from inland. In return for this Turkish help, he promised Aruj free use of the port, with no conditions of tithe attached, and all the facilities ashore that he might need for his men and ships." Possibly Aruj had it in mind that, before very long, he would make himself sole ruler of Bougie, but in any case the offer was an attractive one. The town and the port had everything he needed to further his ambitions.

Lying 120 miles east of Algiers, Bougie had long been one of the most important commercial centres on the North African coast. Its natural harbour, sheltering under the great shoulders of Cape Carbon, could accommodate vessels of almost any draught, while it was protected by fine fortifications that had been erected under the Berber Hammad dynasty and later improved under the Hafsites. About 180 miles southeast of the Balearic Islands, it was in an admirable position for commanding the east-west trade route between Spain, the Strait of Gibraltar, and all the central Mediterranean including Italy and Sicily. Therefore it was better suited than Djerba, which, secure though it was as a refuge, was rather too far to the south of the main shipping routes. Bougie had other attractions. Behind it soared the high peaks of Mounts Babor and Tababor, both crowned with fir and cedar—ideal for shipbuilding—while the surrounding countryside, blessed with a high rainfall, was rich in every kind of vegetable, fruit, and cereal crop. Djerba might, and did, make a fine lair for a corsair, but Bougie was a city and a port fit for a king. Aruj saw himself in this role, and wasted no time in agreeing to the exiled ruler's suggestion.

That summer, while the men in the forts and watchtowers scattered along the coasts of Sicily and Italy gazed anxiously seaward, expecting the annual visitation that was becoming almost as regular as the flights of migratory birds, Aruj and Khizr and their followers were busy with other things. Guns removed from captured galleys had to be provided with suitable carriages for use as siege weapons, and secured in the galleots for the passage to Bougie. Ammunition and gunpowder had to be secured, soldiers adequately armed for land warfare, and provisions laid in for a campaign that might last several weeks. The watchers along the coastlines of the Kingdoms of Naples and Sicily were happy to report that the sea wolves were not in evidence that year.

It was in the month of July that the completed squadron with its siege train and its troops put the island of Djerba behind them. There were twelve galleots, "well provided, having on board 1000 Turks, some Moors, adventurers, and sufficient cannon." The Spanish chronicler Haedo in his *History of Algiers* accounts for the presence of so many Turks by the fact that "Barbarossa's great reputation, and the desire of partaking of Western riches, had enticed [them] down from the Levant, with a thirst not unlike that which hurries us Spaniards to the mines of America."

Following the coast around from Djerba to the Bay of Bougie, the squadron had nearly five hundred miles of rowing ahead of them. But sometimes, when the easterlies blew (not uncommon on that coast in midsummer), they were able to set the lateens and rest easy at the oars. Undoubtedly they called at Tunis to complete their victualling and to rewater, as well as to stock up with further ammunition supplies from the powder mills established outside the town. Their reception by the Sultan of Tunis was more than friendly, for he—like every Moslem ruler—wished to see the hated Spaniards ejected from North Africa, and a ruler installed who was allied by blood and religion to his own house. At a cruising speed of 1½ to 2 knots, together with their short stay in the city, the voyage from Djerba to Bougie must have taken them about fourteen days.

In the hot still month of August, when mirages flickered over the land and when the mountains behind Bougie shook under the summer sun, Aruj Barbarossa led his invasion force down into the bay. He and his brother landed and conferred with their ally, whom they found impatiently awaiting them together with three thousand mountain troops. There was no time to waste, for if the siege should prove a protracted one, the Turkish force would be compelled to retire before the violent changes of weather usually to be expected along that coast in autumn. In any case, they had every confidence that the small Spanish garrison would not be able to resist their combined forces for long.

The cannon were landed, the stone, marble, and iron cannon balls were trundled ashore from the galleys designated as supply ships, and the siege began. Since the discovery of gunpowder contemporaneously by the Englishman Roger Bacon and the German Berthold Schwartz in the fourteenth century, the whole aspect of war had changed. Gone were the great siege engines,

43

giant catapults, and stone-hurling implements that had dominated European warfare since antique times. Nevertheless, the object of the new cannon remained the same as that of the earlier weapons: to open a breach in the walls and permit the armed soldiery to storm in and take the city by hand-to-hand fighting.

A mixture of approximately 66 per cent saltpetre, 22 per cent charcoal, and 12 per cent sulphur was the recipe for most European gunpowders. Loose powder was used for the cannons, while a method had been discovered for hand firearms of mixing the three ingredients wet—"incorporating"—which resulted in a more or less granulated explosive powder, known in England as "corned" powder. The Turks had successfully followed their European neighbours into this new world of high explosives and had made most successful use of them in their capture of Constantinople in 1453. No doubt most of the gunpowder and shot brought by Aruj for the siege of Bougie derived either from Turkish sources—possibly through his trader brother Elias back in Lesbos—or from captured European galleys. Turkish gunnery was soon to become famous on the battlefields of Europe, and the conduct of their gunners in this particular attack showed that they had already developed considerable skill in their craft.

Despite the fact that the fort occupied by the Spaniards had been largely rebuilt and strengthened by Count Don Pedro Navarro when he had captured the town, it was little more than a guard fort designed to protect the shipping and dominate the townspeople. It was not sufficiently strong to resist a prolonged bombardment by heavy cannon. Even so, it withstood a steady battering for seven days, and it was not until the eighth that a breach began to open in the outer walls. Despite their recent reverses at sea, Spanish morale was high at this time. Spaniards were aware of themselves as citizens of a rich country with a great new national pride, and they were among the finest soldiers in Europe. Even with the walls crumbling and a breach established, they had no intention of surrendering. Well armed and well disciplined, they awaited the expected onslaught. On their commander's instructions they held their fire until the massing Turks and hillsmen were committed to the charge and were well within the range of the Spanish arquebuses.

Aruj, whose bravery could never be questioned (even if his impetuosity was to lead him into trouble), was not prepared to wait for a further day's cannonading which would certainly have opened a wide breach, and possibly demoralised the defenders. As soon as he saw that there was room enough for a determined group to launch a frontal assault, he gave the order for the attack and stormed in at the head of his men.

The Spaniards made no move until the attackers had begun scrambling up the broken rubble slope towards the gaping hole in the wall. They then opened fire systematically and coolly upon the onrushing Turks and Zouaves. Courage and headstrong impetuosity are not enough in warfare. Although they may sometimes win battles, they are rarely a match for disciplined intelligence. In those first few volleys, the front ranks of the advancing attackers were decimated, and in one of them, "As Barbarossa was leading his men to the attack, a shot took away his left arm, above the elbow."

It is quite probable that if the Turks had ignored their fallen leader and pressed on, they would still have overwhelmed the defenders (the arquebus was slow to reload), but Aruj Barbarossa's fall demoralised them. In those days the individual leader was all-important. They wavered and hung back; then, picking up their wounded—among them the stricken Aruj—they fled out of range of the Spanish fire. The attack was called off. The disconsolate Turks, Moors, Berbers, and Zouaves withdrew, some to the ships, and the others—including the ex-ruler of Bougie—back to their lair in the mountains.

This was the first big setback experienced by Aruj in his career on the North African coast. To further pursue the parallel careers of this great warrior and seaman with that of Sir Francis Drake, it is interesting to note that Drake and his men suffered a very similar reverse, at a moment when victory seemed within their grasp, exactly sixty years later. In 1572, at the head of a small body of Devonian seamen, Drake had stormed the Spanish city of Nombre de Dios, captured the main square, and had the city at his mercy. At that moment a volley from the Spanish arquebusiers killed and wounded some of the English and Drake was hit in the leg. He lost so much blood "that it soon filled the very prints which our footsteps made, to the great dismay of all our company, who thought it not credible that one should be able to lose so much blood and live." Their leader's disablement had exactly the same effect on Drake's seamen as did that of Aruj Barbarossa on his Turks—they abandoned the attack.

No surgeons were carried aboard the galleots, and indeed there were few enough with surgical knowledge in all Africa. But at Tunis there were skilled Arab physicians (as skilled as any in the world at that time). While the rest of the fleet embarked the soldiers and siege train, one galleot, with a picked crew of Turkish oarsmen, sped back along the coast to Tunis. It carried the unconscious Aruj, with the stump of his left arm constricted by a primitive tourniquet.

Only one stroke of fortune redeemed this first Bougie expedition from disaster. As Khizr Barbarossa and his eleven ships were coasting back towards Tunis they came across a Genoese galleot. She was well to the south of her course, being bound for the island of Tabarka near Alicante Bay in southern Spain. The galleot belonged to the rich Genoese family of Lomellini who owned Tabarka and its coral fisheries, and she was deep-laden with jewellery and other treasure. Captured with hardly any opposition, the galleot was towed back to Tunis where Aruj lay, slowly recovering from the amputation of his arm. But if the Turks and the Sultan of Tunis reckoned that the Genoese galleot was some recompense for the failure of their attack on Bougie, they little realised what a hornet's nest they had stirred up for themselves.

5

THE REVENGE OF
GENOA

The Genoese were not unfamiliar with the name of Barbarossa, nor with the fact that in recent years the coastlines of Italy and Sicily had been under constant attack by him, and that numbers of ships belonging to the King of Spain had never reached their destinations. But the problems of Spain were not their concern. Genoa, in any case, was at this time under French domination. Both Louis XII of France and his heir presumptive, the future Francis I, were very little disturbed at finding that their Spanish enemies were harassed by the Moslems. On the contrary, anything that weakened Spain was to the benefit of France. But that the trade of Genoa should now become a prey to these Barbary corsairs was another matter altogether.

Although Genoa had never really recovered from the blow in 1380 when her fleet under Admiral Luciano Doria had been destroyed in the Venetian lagoons, she was still the second naval power in the Mediterranean. The Venetians might have the largest European shipping fleet in the eastern Mediterranean and the Levant, but Genoa still commanded most of the western trade. It was not for nothing that the city was known as "Genoa the

Superb." Her senate was immediately determined that these sea raiders from North Africa should be taught to discriminate between Genoese shipping and that of other Mediterranean countries.

They had to their hand an efficient instrument, if one may call an instrument a man who was as haughty as Genoa itself—and a great deal more independent. This was the distinguished *condottiere* and soldier of fortune Andrea Doria. He was a descendant of the luckless Luciano, but considerably more able and talented. Born in 1468, he had been early left an orphan and had taken to the profession of arms—the only one suitable for his ancestry and his impecuniosity—before he was twenty. By 1512 he was a mature sea captain of forty-four and an experienced commander of land forces (the two professions being largely indistinguishable at that period). Summoned before the senate, Andrea Doria was ordered to take twelve galleys of the Republic and extirpate the nest of pirates that was lodged in the Goletta of Tunis.

It was late in the year, and there seems little doubt that the Turks were taken totally by surprise when the Genoese squadron of large galleys lifted over the horizon and darted straight for the harbour. Aruj was still too weak from his wound to be able to take any part, so the leadership fell upon Khizr. It was his first encounter with Andrea Doria. The Turkish ships were all inside the harbour when the Genoese anchored offshore and landed a large body of troops. Khizr did the best that he could, sank six of his galleots in the harbour to prevent the enemy from seizing them and towing them away, and sallied out with the remaining six to give battle.

But a galleot, however efficient, was no match for a large galley, manned by disciplined troops and equipped with heavy cannon. Khizr and his men were routed. They beached their ships, and took to their heels inland. Andrea Doria's triumph was complete. His troops landed en masse, drove the Turks back within the walls of Tunis, captured the fort guarding the Goletta and razed it to the ground. They then took the six galleots that had been abandoned, as well as the one captured from them by Khizr, and towed them back in triumph to Genoa. They had inflicted a severe defeat upon "these insolent Moslem pirates." They had, as far as they could see, seized all their ships, and had undoubtedly taught them a lesson—not to interfere with Genoese shipping in the future. Andrea Doria was hailed as a hero of his country and in the following year, 1513, was rewarded by being made Commander of the Galleys of Genoa.

Aruj fumed in impotent fury: half the ships lost, the fortress destroyed, their one prize of the year recaptured, and the Sultan of Tunis beginning to get apprehensive about his policy of permitting the Barbarossas to make use of his port and territory. But there was nothing Aruj could do until his wound was healed, and it was over a year before he was sufficiently recovered to take the warpath again. Khizr, meanwhile, sensing not only the temper of his brother but also that of the Sultan, wisely withdrew to Djerba. He raised the sunken galleots and took them with him, as well as a great deal of shipbuilding material and a number of Christian slaves belonging to him and his brother.

Throughout the winter Khizr and his Turks were steadily engaged on making good their losses. By the spring they had built three new galleots, bringing their numbers up to nine, and they had also established a powder mill on Djerba, so that they were no longer dependent on outside sources for their ammunition supplies. During the following year, 1513, the trade routes of the Mediterranean were unmolested, and the island ports and harbours of the European powers were able to return to normal. The Genoese, it was widely rumoured, had broken the power of the Turkish raiders and had taught them a lesson: not to interfere in the central and western Mediterranean.

But, far south in Djerba, there was no respite from activity. Day and night the shipbuilders and their slave-labour force were kept busy. Aruj himself, almost recuperated from his wound, came down to see his brother Khizr. He forgave him his defeat off Tunis, because of the way in which he had already rebuilt the fleet. Abbot Diego de Haedo, however, who knew many of the younger Barbarossa's servants and followers, says that there was nothing to forgive: that Khizr, under the circumstances in which he was placed when Andrea Doria arrived off the port, did "all that was humanly possible for a man to do."

Aruj was a stubborn man and he was unaccustomed to reverses. Bougie had been almost in his hands when the accident of his wound had caused his men to abandon the attack. He was determined to return the very next year and secure Bougie for himself. He was already in communication with the exiled king, and they had agreed to repeat the plan that had so nearly succeeded in 1512. The Turks would bring the same number of ships, twelve galleots, and the same number of men, and they would once again besiege the city in concert with the mountain troops. What had failed once would surely succeed a second time.

Accordingly, in August 1514, the Spanish garrison at Bougie found itself once again besieged and under fire, and cut off by hostile tribesmen from the interior. "The battery against that unlucky fort was instantly erected, and carried on incessantly with the utmost fury. In a very few days he almost levelled it with the ground, and the Spaniards, forced to dislodge, retired to the city . . ." Bougie was now protected by a further bastion, which had been erected in the past two years. It stood on the edge of the sea, "whose strand and shore," Morgan comments, "is very beautiful." It was indeed a lovely stretch of coast, with mountains rising behind it and with fertile land running down to the sea. But this rich agricultural land, combined with yet another stroke of ill-fortune, was to help deprive the Turks once again of their anticipated victory.

As August drew to a close, the clouds began to mass above the mountains. The rainy season was approaching, and while the siege of the second bastion went ahead the first rains of September started to fall. Now the Berbers, and especially the coast-dwelling Moors, were entirely dependent upon this autumn rainfall for their next year's crops. It was imperative for them to get back to their farms and small holdings, "in order to plough and sow their lands, for the best sowing time in Barbary is after the first rains have fallen." Gradually the ground forces began to slink away. It was at this very moment, when once again the city of Bougie seemed to lie within their grasp, that Aruj and Khizr were told by their coastal lookouts that Spanish ships were approaching.

It was the annual autumn relief, bringing with it ammunition and stores to enable the garrison to survive through the winter. Under the command of a Spanish captain, Martin de Renteria, five large men-of war—sailing galleons that took advantage of a fine onshore breeze—came proudly into the bay. They had with them, though the Barbarossas did not as yet know it, several companies of land troops designed to replace the garrison. Deprived of his land support by the rapid desertion of the Moors and Berbers, and threatened from the sea by a force considerably stronger and better armed than his own, Aruj was once again compelled to raise the siege. "He is said to have departed like one frantic, tearing his beard for mere madness, to find himself so baffled and disappointed."

He refused to go back to Djerba, for he still felt that although the island had already proved its worth as a refuge and a place in which to recoup his losses, it was too far away from the main stream of western Mediterranean trade. Tunis also was out of the question, for to return to Tunis baffled a second time in an attempt on Bougie would be to court a strong rebuff from the Sultan. The latter was already deeply worried that the activities of the Turks would result in the destruction of his city at the hands of the Genoese.

On his two passages along the coast Aruj had already noted the small peninsula of Djidjelli sticking its craggy beak out into the sea, some forty miles to the east from Bougie. Possibly he had landed there on one or other occasion to water his ships. Certainly he knew that there was a harbour perfectly adequate for his galleots on the eastern side of the peninsula: a harbour protected by an off-lying islet, and fringed with rocks and shoals. The town itself was perched high above, and was almost inaccessible by frontal assault. From the rear, if its defences were improved, it was clear that the whole peninsula could be turned into an excellent fortress. There were no more than one thousand inhabitants, sturdy Berber farmers, who owed no allegiance to any Sultan, and who were more than happy to see the Turkish vessels in their harbour, bringing with them trade and a steady demand for their agricultural produce.

So in late September 1514, just in time to avoid the beginning of the stormy autumn season along the North African coast, Aruj and Khizr Barbarossa brought their twelve ships and their 1,100 Turks into the harbour of Djidjelli. Together with them there were several hundred Moors, as well as other adventurers who had joined their force for the assault on Bougie. The very fact that Aruj chose Djidjelli as his base, so near to the scene of his recent rebuff, suggests that he still had it in mind to attempt Bougie again at the first opportunity.

It was, according to Haedo, a hard autumn that year along that part of the coast, and the addition of so many mouths to feed in the small town and harbour soon meant that some sort of rationing had to be imposed. The Barbarossas, however, were careful to see that the native inhabitants were well treated by their men. If they needed to have a port at their backs, they knew how important it was that the people in their base should be their friends. If not, when they took to the sea again in spring, they might well return to find that their refuge had been betrayed behind them to the Spaniards.

As often happens in the Mediterranean, the weather which had been so harsh throughout September and October suddenly fined down in November to give days of cloudless calm. The Turkish captains knew that such weather might well last into mid or even late December, before the winter proper settled down over land and sea. There was just a chance—and Aruj and Khizr took it—of catching some "late swallows" on the wing between Spain and her domains in Naples and Sicily.

All twelve galleots, having taken aboard water and supplies, headed up into the Mediterranean. They spread themselves across the main shipping lane between Sicily, Sardinia, the Balearic Islands, and Spain. It took them nearly three days to reach their chosen station, about 125 miles from Djidjelli. Once there, they positioned themselves like a seine net across the sea. If each galleot can be regarded as something like the glass float that supports a seine net (each bobbing within sight of one another), it is easy to see how twelve ships, stationed on the idle autumn sea, could command a large area. From a height of ten feet above the water, the distance of the sea horizon to a captain on the aft steering deck of a small galleot would be little more than 3½ miles. But he could always send a lookout aloft up the mainmast, and increase his horizon distance to double this. Assuming that the Turkish vessels worked somewhere between these two points, it is likely that they cruised about five miles apart, moving eastwards into the Sardinia-Sicily strait. Twelve galleys, therefore, could easily cover a sea lane of sixty miles. The Barbarossas knew that it was in the area sixty to seventy miles south of Cape Spartivento, at the extreme southern tip of

Sardinia, that they would find what they were looking for—merchantmen making the last run of the season back to Spain with corn from Sicily.

"So, our corsair went on a cruise, with all his twelve galleots, towards Sardinia and Sicily, to try if he could pick up any barques laden with corn, or other provisions . . ." Some might say that they were lucky, but luck plays a comparatively small part in the career of a successful man of action. Luck is needed, certainly, but the prime requisites are intelligence and a first-class knowledge of the world in which he operates. Within a few days the galleots had netted three large merchantmen moving slowly homeward to Spain.

The ships they captured were almost certainly of the type known as a galleasse—a transitional design between the oared-galley proper and the sailing merchantship. Some idea of the size of these ships can be gauged from the fact that the Portuguese and Spanish galleasses of this period usually carried over one hundred soldiers, and over two hundred galley slaves to work the oars. They did, indeed, carry guns with which to defend themselves, but they were primarily cargo-carrying merchantships. They might be compared, perhaps, to the merchantmen of the last two World Wars which had a few guns and trained crews to man them, but whose real duty was to transport cargo.

Towing their three prizes behind them, the Turkish galleots walked casually back on their long legs of oars across the peaceful sea. They arrived at Djidjelli well before the storms of winter broke. By their successful action they had not only secured their own winter provisions, they had also gained the affection of the local inhabitants. "Out of this seasonable supply he [Aruj] made such liberal distributions among the hungry Djidjellians, and the neighbouring mountaineers . . . that he won their affections to such a degree that his word became a law and an oracle."

Aruj was never as intelligent as his younger brother, Khizr, but there can be little doubt that it was upon the well-based pragmatism of Aruj that the latter was to secure his later successes. He took great care to "cultivate and improve this mighty opinion that the natives had conceived of him; and had the address so well to manage matters that these indomitable mountain Africans, who all along had preferred their liberty against the powerful kings of Tunis and others . . . proclaimed him their Sovereign, with the royal title of Sultan."

Aruj now found himself the ruler of what was at any rate a first-class seaport—due south of the main western Mediterranean trading routes—and without obligation to any local king or sheikh. The year that had seemed to promise a kingdom in Bougie, and that had gone so ill with the desertion of his native troops and the arrival of the Spanish reinforcements, had ultimately ended well for the Barbarossas. Their ships were hauled ashore out of reach of the winter storms, their slaves were housed in rock quarries beneath the town, and they had security in which to plan for the insecurity of others.

6

SULTAN OF ALGIERS

Next spring Aruj Barbarossa consolidated his position. Taking the field at the head of his own men and of his new subjects, he administered a smart defeat upon a Zouave tribe under their king, Aben al Cadi. The latter was killed, his head brought back in triumph to adorn the walls of Djidjelli, and "the reputation of this victory was such that several mountains came under Barbarossa's obedience."

It is worth noting that the whole pattern of Aruj's life is remote from that of a typical pirate or corsair. Both the Barbarossas did, indeed, raid the shipping lanes of the enemies of their country and their faith, but always with the object of using the captured shipping and materials to secure for themselves a land kingdom. They became pirates, in fact, in order to secure a "working capital." With the aid of this capital they invested in cannon and troops. These were no simple pirates like the Europeans who would later haunt the Caribbean—sailors or criminals who "went on the account" because it provided a means of earning a living. The actions of the Barbarossas must always be seen in this context—that, though both brothers were great seamen, they used the sea in order to establish themselves upon the land.

The Mediterranean had long been haunted by pirates, using the term in its proper sense: Italian, Greek, Turkish, and Moorish renegade mariners, who preyed upon shipping and then retired to their hideouts to digest like boa constrictors until such time as they needed a further "meal." Neither Aruj nor Khizr fell into this simple category, even in their early days. Their depredations in the Mediterranean were certainly far in excess of anything achieved by traditional pirates, for the reason that they were carried out with intelligence and always with an objective. To carry the analogy into terms of modern strategy and warfare, the Barbarossas had a political objective behind their military or naval excursions. The true pirate, like the inefficient commander in war, has always been something of a failure because he has had no political objective, only the immediate object of conquest and material gain.

For the whole of that year Aruj and Khizr maintained their headquarters in Djidjelli, going out on a cruise to restock their larder before winter. It is unlikely that any important prizes were taken, for the records of the year 1515 do not contain any complaints by European powers about the rapacity of the Turkish pirates. But, within the next few months, Aruj was to be offered the opportunity to acquire that land kingdom which he had always wanted.

"A.D. 1516. This year, died Don Ferdinand, further named the Catholic, aged sixty-two years. The people of Algiers, whom, for nearly seven years, he had held in such subjection by the fort he built on the little island, that they not only paid him tribute, but even durst not peep their heads out of the harbour, nor repair their decaying row-boats, much less build new ones: And if they had, to what purpose? They had early news of the death of his Catholic Majesty, and thought then, or never to free themselves . . ." King Ferdinand died late in January, and as soon as the news reached North Africa, the Algerians called upon the neighbouring Arab ruler, Sheikh Selim, to help rid them of the Spanish garrison. This garrison dominated the city from a fortress erected on the island at the mouth of the port, and thus prevented the Algerians from either trading legitimately or indulging in piratical forays upon the Spanish shipping lanes.

Selim was willing to undertake the blockade of the Spaniards from the land, but was well aware that he had neither the cannon nor the equipment to undertake a siege. There was one man, however, whose name was now known throughout the whole coast and who, although twice worsted at Bougie, had shown that he and his troops understood the art of siege warfare. Selim sent an envoy to Aruj in Djidjelli, inviting him and his Turks to participate in the liberation of Algiers. Nothing could have suited the elder Barbarossa better. Algiers would make an even finer conquest than Bougie. It was the most important and populous city on the coast, with an excellent harbour, and from its situation due south of Mallorca it seemed designed by nature to command the east-west shipping routes of the western Mediterranean.

Having accepted Sheikh Selim's invitation, Aruj sent sixteen galleots down the coast, "most of them his own, with 500 Turks, some artillery and all necessaries." These were under his brother's command, while Aruj himself marched for Algiers with 800 Turks, 3000 of his local subjects, and 2000 other Moorish volunteers. Selim and his followers met him a day's march out of Algiers, but were disappointed to find that Barbarossa was not coming to the immediate relief of the city. Aruj had every intention of attacking the Spanish garrison, but first of all he had a little personal business to settle. About forty-five miles west of Algiers lies the small port of Shershell, where another Turkish sea rover, Kara Hassan, had (like Aruj in Djidjelli) made himself the local Sultan. He had also attracted under his command a great number of Moors, as well as Turks, together with their galleots. Aruj needed these men and their ships, and he wanted also to secure his western flank prior to attacking Algiers. There was no room in Barbarossa's philosophy for two Turkish rulers on the North African coast.

Kara Hassan was tricked into believing that Aruj had come to solicit his help, but before he had time to realise his mistake, he felt the wind of the corsair's scimitar. "This execution done, he [Barbarossa] hastened to take possession of his late legacy; and without more ado forced all the Turks he found there to list into his service, and caused himself to be proclaimed Sultan, or King of Shershell, and its small dominion."

The Spanish chronicler Haedo refers to the murder of Kara Hassan as "this barbarous cruelty," but Morgan in his *History of Algiers* concedes that "some would call it state-policy." Certainly the act was infamous by modern standards (when political rivals are usually assassinated by word rather than deed), yet in terms of the sixteenth century Aruj was no more cynically murderous than many of the Italian princes and *condottieri* who have attracted European admiration. In any event, the act was certainly statesmanlike, for Aruj was now the master of a town and harbour on either flank of Algiers. Even if he were to fail now against the city, he would be in an admirable position to exert a pincers movement upon it and its territory at a future date.

Leaving a garrison of his own men, a personally selected band who could be trusted to hold Shershell for him and not to get ambitious on their own account, Aruj now swung right and marched up the coast. Arriving off Algiers he and his men were welcomed into the town by Sheikh Selim, and Aruj undertook the siege of the garrison.

But on this occasion his comparatively light cannons were

inadequate for the reduction of a fortress that had been designed to resist heavy siege guns. Almost certainly Aruj Barbarossa had some inkling of this before he began the attack, for he sent a messenger across to the Spanish commander offering him and his troops a free passage if they would submit. Courage was something that the Spaniards never lacked, and back came the swift answer: "Neither your threats, nor your proffered courtesies, can have any effect upon men like us—although they might perhaps work upon cowards. But don't forget what happened at Bougie—you may come off even worse here!"

On receipt of this contemptuous reply Aruj opened the siege. For twenty days his guns played upon the walls and defences of the island fort, but without making enough impression to open a breach in the walls. Realising that he was unlikely to be able to dislodge the garrison until he had really heavy ordnance at his command, Aruj decided that the time had come to make himself master of Algiers. Once this was done, he would be able to subdue the Spanish garrison at his leisure.

Sheikh Selim and his followers now found that they had made the mistake of the frogs in the fable, and merely exchanged King Log for King Stork. The fate of Kara Hassan should perhaps have warned them that a Turk like Barbarossa might indeed be a fellow Moslem, but he was first and foremost a Turk. Events in Egypt and other parts of the Moslem world were soon to show the Arabic peoples that their Turkish coreligionists were intent on establishing a vast empire—and whether they carved it out of Europe or the Middle East did not greatly matter to them. "Allah," as an Arabic proverb runs, "has an army which he has named the Turks. Whenever he is angry with a people, he lets loose his army upon them." Allah, as events were to prove, was just as likely to be angry with a Moslem people as with Christians.

There are two versions of the way in which Sheikh Selim met

his end. One suggests that he retired with his followers to the mountains, and was lured down by Barbarossa to a meeting "where, instantly at his arrival . . . he was caused to be hanged in his own turban, at the eastern gate of the city." This is the version given by the Spanish writer Marmol, but the Abbot Diego de Haedo provides the following account, which in many respects sounds more typical of the elder Barbarossa. "As Barbarossa's thoughts were day and night employed in contriving how to make himself master of the place [Algiers], he at length resolved to put his project into execution. The better to bring it about, without noise or tumult, one day, about noon, as Sheikh Selim was bathing alone, in order to prepare himself for the Mosque, he [Barbarossa] slily entered the Prince's bath, or Bagnio, within the palace, accompanied by only one Turk, where the poor Prince, who, naked and defenceless, mistrusting no treachery, was by them easily surprised and strangled with a wet towel, or napkin." It was then given out that he had succumbed to a stroke in the heat of the bath. Too late the dismayed Algerians discovered that their new "protector" had his own interests at heart long before anything else, and that he was likely to be a more imperious Sultan than any who had reigned in the city for many years.

Aruj's first act was to start repairing and fortifying the Casbah against the day when, having eliminated the Spanish garrison, he would be able to dominate Algiers from his own fortress. He had himself formally proclaimed Ruler or Sultan of Algiers, and instructed the mint to issue money, both gold and silver, on which was stamped in Turkish characters "Sultan Aruj." Meanwhile the citizens were made miserably aware of the presence of the Spanish garrison. Prior to the arrival of the Turks, there had been an unwritten agreement between the Spaniards and the Algerians that, provided the latter conducted themselves well and did not try to engage in piracy, they would be left alone. But the presence of Turkish troops in the town, and of Barbarossa's ships off the port, activated the garrison into a bombardment of the city. The Algerians found themselves unable to conduct any business, while at the same time their houses and their families were under constant threat from the Spanish gunners.

They decided that the devil they knew was infinitely preferable to this devil whom they were reluctantly beginning to know only too well. Messages were secretly exchanged with the garrison, and a plot was hatched to lure the Turks outside the walls and massacre them. Barbarossa's galleots, now twenty-two in number (having been joined by the former followers of Kara Hassan), were all beached ashore out of range of the fortress's guns. The Algerians' plan was simple: to set fire to the galleots and then, when the Turks rushed down to save their vessels, to shut the gate of the city against them. At the same time the Spanish troops were to embark in some small boats that they had ready on the island and cross to the mainland. Together with the fighting men of the town and a band of Arab cavalry from the hinterland, they would fall upon the Turks and cut them to pieces round their ruined boats.

Unfortunately for the Algerians, Aruj had never for a moment trusted them, let alone believed that they found his presence in their city attractive. His spies had infiltrated the leaders of the dissident citizens, and he had every detail of the plot to hand long before it was ready to be put into execution. So on the day selected for setting fire to the galleots, the Algerians who had been chosen for the task found to their dismay that every vessel was guarded by a band of armed Turks, who afforded a simple, and reasonable, explanation for their presence: "Sultan Aruj was worried that possibly the Spanish garrison might make an attempt upon our ships."

Foiled in their plan, the Algerians were in a desperate position, for they did not know—but could only suspect—how well the Barbarossas were acquainted with their plot. Aruj bided his time, did nothing to show that he mistrusted any of the leading citizens, and "artfully dissembled, making not the least show of mistrust." But on the Moslem sabbath, the Friday following the attempt on his ships, Aruj and Khizr went with their close circle of followers to the main mosque in Algiers, theoretically to perform their devotions. Aruj knew that all the chief citizens, and among them the ringleaders in the plot, would inevitably be present on such an occasion. When all the Algerians had entered the mosque they were startled to hear the clash of the great wooden doors behind them, and to find that at every door stood a body of armed Turks.

Aruj now addressed the congregation, as it were; told them that he had anticipated their designs against him, and that he had little or no use for men who were prepared to trade and act in concert with the hated Christians in order to save their own lives and property. Trembling with fear, the imprisoned Arabs and Moors of Algiers heard him out—this red-bearded, broad-shouldered tyrant who had suddenly come to trouble their comparatively easy peace with the Spaniards.

His cool discourse concluded, Aruj made a motion with his hand, and a second later his Turks were moving amongst the assembled faithful. All were bound, "using their own turbans," and then a selected few—names that Aruj had learned through his agents—were taken to the main door of the mosque. Twenty men, according to the most reliable authority, were hauled outside. There, in front of the terrified people in the street, their heads were struck from their shoulders and their bodies left to lie in the dust, under the summer sun, with the swarming flies of Algeria buzzing over the black blood round the severed trunks. Aruj now turned upon the rest of the silent and bound company, and told them that, for their own security, it would be best if they co-operated with him. As Sultan of Algiers he needed money in order to improve the city and make good its defences against the Christians. He intended to make Algiers the supreme city in North Africa. Naturally, as leading citizens, they would be only too willing to invest in such a sensible and profitable enterprise. There were no dissentients.

Sultan and ruler of Djidjelli to the east, Shershell to the west, and now of Algiers, the elder Barbarossa was a formidable figure in the Mediterranean. In the space of six years, despite two major reverses, he had carved out an Ottoman empire on shores that had hitherto been dominated by Arabs, Berbers, or Spaniards. He had laid the foundations of a North African power that was to trouble all Europe for over three centuries.

7

THE DEATH OF
ARUJ

In May 1517 a galleot came scudding into Algiers with the news
that a powerful Spanish fleet was on its way to attack the city.
Rumours of activity in Spain during the winter had already
reached Aruj, for there was a steady flow of intelligence between
the Moriscos in Spain and their brothers on the North African
coast. Admiral Diego de Vera, one of Spain's most distinguished
fighting men, at the instigation of Cardinal Ximenes of Toledo,
had brought out the most powerful elements of the Spanish fleet.
Together with a force of some ten thousand soldiers, he intended
to cure finally and forever this running sore on the flank of
Spain. It was unthinkable that the might of the greatest European power should any longer be mocked, let alone challenged,
by a handful of Turks and dissident Moors on the bare North
African coast. There could, he must have felt, be no doubt about
the outcome.

Aruj and Khizr and their Turkish followers were not unpre-
pared for the attack. Part of the Spanish plan hinged on the
participation of local forces, who had been incited to rise against
the Turks by the son of the murdered Selim, eager to revenge his

father's death. But now that Shershell and other areas west of Algiers were under Barbarossa's rule, he had, as it were, excellent listening posts to protect his flank on the side towards Oran and the towns and ports that were still under Spanish domination.

The Spanish war galleys hovered around the transports to protect them, while the latter backed in under oars towards the coast and ran out their landing stages. Troops and horses streamed ashore for the assault on the city. But Aruj was never dilatory. As an able commander, he well knew that the moment to strike an enemy landing force is when it is in the process of getting ashore and re-forming. At the head of his Turkish brigade, backed by mounted troops from the interior, he swept down on the beachhead. Diego de Vera, however competent he may have previously proved himself in the Spanish war against France, seems to have had little knowledge of the hazards involved in a sea-borne invasion. Although he immediately attempted to throw up trenches around his beachhead, he was too late. Aruj and his men, sweeping down from the hillside overlooking the invasion area, cut the Spaniards to pieces.

As Sandoval, Bishop of Pamplona, commented in his *History of Charles V:* "One day Barbarossa came out, noticed that the Spaniards were in poor array, and fell upon them with his forces shouting war cries. So great was the fear that his very name inspired that the Spaniards were totally routed, with very little loss to the attackers. Almost effortlessly the Turks and their followers killed over 3000 men as well as capturing 400." The small number of prisoners is unusual, and it may mean that the Turks, contrary to their normal practice, were bent on slaughter rather than the capture of potential slaves. On the other hand, it may only be a proof that the soldiers of Spain, always among the bravest in the world, refused to yield, and so were cut down without mercy on the hostile shore. Despairingly the galleys and transports backed and filled off the coast, totally unable to help their stricken comrades—for they could not risk their ships falling into enemy hands if they were to beach themselves in an attempt to evacuate the army.

A disaster for Spain, a triumph for Aruj—such was the outcome of the great expedition of 1517. As if to ensure the ruin of the Spaniards, the weather now blew foul. A sudden storm sprang up towards nightfall and drove many of the ships ashore. It is possible that they had made a last-minute attempt to evacuate what was left of their ruined army. Sailing vessels of that period, caught on a lee shore, had little or no hope of ever clawing windward to safety. Even well-manned galleys could make little headway against a heavy wind and sea. Discounting one report which says that "almost the whole Armada was totally destroyed," there can be no doubt that the damage to the ships, as well as loss of life, was considerable. When Admiral Diego de Vera finally staggered homeward to Spain, he left Aruj Barbarossa undisputed master of the coast.

According to Haedo, "his good fortune on this occasion greatly enhanced his reputation, firmly establishing him in rulership. He was, indeed, looked upon as something of a prodigy . . ." Not the man to miss such an opportunity, with the enemy's fleet in ruins and so many Spanish soldiers dead, captured, or returned to Spain with shattered morale, Aruj summoned out the galleots. A cloud of them, under Khizr and other leading corsairs, descended suddenly upon the coasts of Spain, burning, harrying, looting, carrying off slaves, and bringing back freed Moriscos to join their own forces.

In June that same year, the ruler of Tenez, a fair-sized city and port about ninety miles west of Algiers, raised the countryside against the Turks and marched eastwards against them. His own force is said to have consisted of ten thousand regular troops, backed up by local cavalry, while many of the mountain tribes who acknowledged his sovereignty joined in to swell his numbers. Many of the Moors, Arabs, and other inhabitants of North Africa were already beginning to realise that the Turks represented a far greater threat to their independence and to their established way of life than did the Spaniards. The latter, after all, were only concerned with maintaining garrisons at fixed points along the coast, and had shown no desire to extend their empire into North Africa proper. But it was already clear in what direction the Turks' ambitions were moving. It was also abundantly clear that so long as there were Turkish forces on the coastline the Spaniards would be unlikely to leave North Africa in peace.

Aruj wasted no time, but set off immediately to meet his enemies in the field. Algiers could almost certainly have resisted a siege, even if his enemies had been armed with cannon. But to sit back and wait for an attack was not in his nature. Leaving Khizr behind to maintain the city, he took about 1500 Turks and Spanish Moors with him, all trained arquebusiers, and marched swiftly westwards to catch his opponents just as they were crossing a small river. Against the trained marksmen in Aruj's force the hordes of desert cavalry and partially armed foot soldiers from Tenez had little or no chance. They were mown down in their hundreds, and soon the rest were in full flight, the ruler of Tenez amongst them. Again Aruj did not delay, but set off by forced marches after the beaten enemy—entering Tenez itself just as its prince was escaping with his followers to take refuge in the hills. Having given the town over to plunder, Aruj recalled the inhabitants, promised them his protection, and had himself proclaimed Sultan of Tenez.

It was a swift and brilliant campaign; a model of how to conduct a defensive action by immediately taking the offensive. It was clear that quite apart from their advantage in possessing modern weapons, the Turks had no military rivals in North Africa. They possessed the prime requirement of the soldier—an aggressive spirit.

As evidence that this spirit not only wins battles but also wins over any neighbours who may be wavering in their loyalties, a deputation now reached Aruj from Tlemcen. This was an important town and trading post, some seventy miles inland by road from Spanish-dominated Oran. Dissatisfied with their present ruler, the chief citizens offered Tlemcen and its surrounding territory to Aruj if he would help them. Naturally Aruj was far from unwilling—an important city dominating the hinterland and a permanent threat to Oran was much to his taste—but he was not foolhardy. Knowing that the Spanish Governor of Oran might well move against him and cut him off from his coastal route to Algiers, he despatched a message to Khizr. The latter was requested to bring round to Tenez by sea ten light cannon, ammunition, and other supplies.

Thus reinforced with cannon that could be used if necessary in a siege, and if not, against troops in the field, Aruj moved rapidly against Tlemcen. It was nearly two hundred miles from Tenez; it was midsummer; and his troops had been almost continually under arms since he had left Algiers in June. It is a tribute to their fitness and their fighting spirit that when they encountered the ruler of Tlemcen together with a force almost three times their own, the Turks were ready for immediate battle. Aruj's foresight in bringing along the field guns was amply rewarded. The native troops, most of whom had never been under cannon fire before, turned and fled. In September 1517 Aruj entered the city of Tlemcen in triumph. In front of him went the head of its late ruler, borne before the conqueror on a lance.

With the exception of Oran and the fortress on the island off Algiers, as well as a few other defence points on the coast, Aruj was now master of almost all the territory that constitutes modern Algeria. With his brother at Algiers in command of the coast, and himself at Tlemcen in command of the interior, the Barbarossas were in a position to deal with any trouble that might arise among the native tribesmen. With a view to securing Tlemcen as his main inland base, Aruj acted as he had done at Algiers: he made sure that the leading citizens contributed not only to his coffers, but also to the defences of their city. During the winter of 1517–18 the citadel and the walls were expanded and renewed, for Aruj was well aware that he might soon have to face an attack mounted by the Spaniards from Oran.

In the meantime, he despatched emissaries to the rulers of Fez and Tunis. He was now in a position to treat with them as an equal. Having made himself Sultan of Middle Barbary, he naturally wished to have friendly relationships on his east and west boundaries. He promised both Fez and Tunis that he would be their ally against their common enemy, the Christians, while he added the additional clause for the ruler of Fez that he would assist him against the latter's main enemy, the King of Morocco. That winter was the high point of Aruj Barbarossa's career. Starting from nothing but two small galleots in 1504, he and a handful of fellow Turks had made themselves a power upon the sea. He himself was now master of a kingdom that was in no way inferior to any in North Africa. Indeed, by concentrating upon the Algerian coastline, he had secured not only one of the most prosperous agricultural areas but the one which was in the best position to harass Spain and dominate the east-west trade route of the Mediterranean. He was now Sultan of Tlemcen, Tenez, and Shershell—and recognised as Ruler of Algiers, with the official title of Beylerbey, by Selim the Grim, Sultan of all the Ottoman Empire. It was no mean achievement.

While the brothers were busy in Tlemcen and Algiers, the Governor of Oran, the Marquis of Comares, had set out for Spain to wait upon the new King, Charles I of Spain (later the

Emperor Charles V). The Marquis pointed out the desperate situation that now obtained in North Africa. The garrison fort in Algiers was virtually cut off, and only Oran was under full Spanish control. "Before the Barbarossa brothers were able to gain complete control of their kingdom," the Marquis urged, "now was surely time to unseat them." In a year or more, they might be virtually unassailable, and they would be in a position to cut off Oran itself by land and sea. Not unnaturally, the seventeen-year-old monarch saw a brilliant opening to his career in extirpating these Turks from the coastline and ports that threatened his country and its trade. Orders were given for an expedition to be prepared over that winter. It was to sail in early spring to secure Oran, and to drive the Turks clean out of the country.

Aruj had word of what was under way, and sent a despatch to the Sultan of Fez asking his help against the Spaniards. He was well aware that he had neither the men, the cannon, nor the equipment to hold out in Tlemcen against a large and disciplined force. But the Sultan prevaricated and delayed. He had his own problems on his Moroccan border. Besides, like other North African rulers, he was not entirely happy with the presence of these Turks, who seemed to have a habit of helping themselves to Sultanates while at the same time provoking the retribution of Spain. When the spring came and the Spanish fleet, with troopships laden with about ten thousand veterans, had reached Oran and disembarked, the Sultan had still failed to send any help to his new ally.

Aruj found himself with 1500 men (his Turkish and Morisco arquebusiers) in Tlemcen, two hundred miles from Algiers, and with a large army advancing inland to lay siege to the city. He was in little doubt that, despite the hard work of the winter, the defences of Tlemcen would not hold out against the siege artillery of the Spaniards. When it was quite clear that there were only two alternatives, to stay and die in Tlemcen, or to retreat,

Aruj set out overnight for Algiers. By forced marches, and using his intimate knowledge of the country, he hoped to break through to the coastal roads and get safely within the walls of Algiers before the Spaniards could catch up with him. For once he had delayed too long. He had, perhaps, made a mistake that he had never in his life made before—he had relied on help from another. It is difficult to believe that he would have delayed so long at Tlemcen if he had not confidently expected reinforcements from the Sultan of Fez to come in from the west and cut off the Spaniards from their base at Oran.

The Marquis of Comares got wind of the Turks' departure from Tlemcen, and knowing that Aruj would certainly march northeast to get through the mountain valleys in the direction of the sea, he swung his forces swiftly in that direction. Leaving some of his infantry to follow on behind, he mounted all he could on captured Moorish horses. Then, together with his regular cavalry, he set off in hot pursuit. He came in sight of the Turks about thirty miles east of Tlemcen. They were heading for a river, one of those precipitous, gorgelike wadis which are often as dry as dust in summer but which still have a good flow of water through them in spring. Aruj quickened his pace in order to reach the far side, from which he might be able to prevent the enemy crossing. It is said that in order to delay the Spaniards he even resorted to that age-old stratagem (first used by Hippomenes, Atalanta's suitor, when he dropped behind him the golden apples of the Hesperides) and scattered in his flight gold, gem stones, and other treasure amassed from Tenez and Tlemcen. This ruse, says the Spanish chronicler somewhat smugly, "might have passed, had it been practised upon any others but Spaniards." But, as Morgan relates, the Spaniards, urged on by the Marquis, "trampled under foot that for which all the world goes by the ears, and soon fell in with the enemy's rear."

Aruj and half of his force had already forded the river and

established themselves on the eastern bank when the Spanish cavalry came up with the Turks who were still descending the further slopes. Aruj was ever a brave man, and he would not stay in safety while the men who had been his companions for many years were being slaughtered. He recrossed the river, gathered them round him, and stationed them on a small hillock that dominated the fording place. There the Turks "turning their faces and breasts to the enemy, like men determined to die bravely" made their last stand. Among them, Aruj, "though he had but one arm, fought to the very last gasp like a lion." It was an end such as a man of his calibre would have sought:

> . . . *Not in curtained solemnity die*
> *Among women who chatter and cry and children*
> *who mumble a prayer.*

So died Aruj Barbarossa, son of a janissary and a Greek woman, born in Lesbos, resident for fourteen years in North Africa, and the founder of the Kingdom of Algiers. Morgan's eighteenth-century English translation catches something of the flavour of Abbot Haedo's tribute, and it must always be remembered that the latter not only knew men who had served with Aruj, was himself a long-time resident in Algiers, but that he was, above all, a Spanish Catholic. This tribute, then, from one who had every reason to detest the Barbarossas, is all the more convincing: "Aruj Barbarossa, according to the testimony of those who remember him, was, when he died, about forty-four years of age. He was not very tall of stature, but extremely well-set and robust. His hair and beard perfectly red; his eyes quick, sparkling and lively; his nose aquiline, or Roman; and his complexion between brown and fair. He was a man excessively bold, resolute, daring, magnanimous, enterprising, profusely liberal, and in no wise bloodthirsty, except when in the heat of battle, nor rigorously cruel except when disobeyed. He was highly beloved, feared and respected by his soldiers and domestics, and when dead was by them all in general most bitterly regretted and lamented. He left neither son nor daughter. He resided in Barbary fourteen years; during which the harms he did to the Christians are inexpressible."

Not all the Turks who had crossed to the far side of the river had Barbarossa's courage and resolution to return and make an end in the company of their comrades. Some of them fought their way back through that harsh and difficult countryside until they reached the safety of Algiers.

The crimson brocade cloak which Aruj was wearing when he was killed was later taken to the episcopal see of Cordova, a city that owes its distinction to the Moorish architects who had dignified and beautified it during their occupation of Spain. Here, in the cathedral which had formerly been the largest sacred building in Islam (except for the Kaaba at Mecca), it was turned into a cloak for Saint Bartholomew. It was still to be seen in the eighteenth century on the saint's image, and was known locally as *La Capa de Barbarossa*. Tlemcen was restored by the Spaniards to a local ruler, on condition that he paid an annual fee of vassalage of 12,000 golden ducats, twelve Arab horses, and six falcons to the King of Spain.

A Spanish lieutenant, Garcia de Tineo, is said to have been the one who finally struck down the old sea wolf with a pike thrust, and afterwards cut off his head. Duro relates that his family were subsequently allowed to incorporate the head of Barbarossa in their coat of arms. Even his enemies considered that Barbarossa was worthy of epic treatment, for he was the subject of an eighteenth-century Spanish heroic poem and, as late as the nineteenth century, of a stage tragedy. The King of Fez did finally arrive to aid his new ally—fifteen days too late. He had with him, according to one account, 20,000 men. However inefficiently armed and undisciplined, it is almost certain that such a force would have been more than enough to cut off the Spaniards from their base at Oran and deliver the whole area safely and forever into Moslem hands. But, hearing on the borders of Algeria what had happened to Aruj and his Turks, "he hastened away for fear of the Spaniards and their allies." "Put not your trust in princes." It was a mistake that cost Aruj his life.

8

WRECK OF A
FLEET

The death of Aruj was a bitter blow to the Turks, but it was by no means the disaster that it would have been had it occurred a few years earlier. They were now firmly established throughout North Africa, from Djerba to Tenez, and the Sultan in Constantinople had already seen what advantages could accrue to his empire by having his left flank in the hands of fellow Turks. There is little doubt that, even before Aruj's death, there had been friendly and regular communications between the Sublime Porte and the Barbarossa brothers. Automatically, the mantle of high command now fell upon the able shoulders of Khizr. He had learned much from his brother in the past fourteen years, and he was soon to show that he had every bit as much aptitude for war, and even more for negotiation, politics, and—ultimately—for statesmanship.

It was to Khizr, then, that the Turks in Algiers looked for advice in the present situation. Even in appearance he was a born leader: "His stature was advantageous; his Mien portly and majestick; well proportioned and robust; very hairy, with a Beard extremely bushy; his Brows and Eye-lashes remarkably long and thick; Before his Hair turned grey and hoary, it was a bright Auburn; so that the Surname Barbarossa, or Red-Beard, was conferred on him, rather to preserve the memory of his Brother Aruj, than from any Title he had to that Appellation . . ."

Barbarossa was, of course, only the nickname by which he— like his brother—was known to Christians. To Turks and fellow Moslems he was to be known in his lifetime and ever since not as Khizr, his baptismal name, but as Kheir-ed-Din—"Protector of Religion." This informal title seems to have been bestowed upon him during the next few years. Certainly it is as Kheir-ed-Din that the records name him during the rest of his life. Kheir-ed-Din might indeed be translated as "Defender of the Faith." It is a curious thought that at about the same time that Khizr Barbarossa acquired this name, King Henry VIII of England received the title "Defender of the Faith" from Pope Leo X (in return for his defence of the papacy against Martin Luther in 1521). But whereas the successors of Leo X were to regret having bestowed such a mistaken epithet upon the "Heretic Henry," Kheir-ed-Din remained a fitting name for Khizr Barbarossa to the end of his days. He was to prove a bastion of the Moslem faith in the Mediterranean Sea, and such a scourge to Christians that he also deserved the name later given to Dragut, one of his chief lieutenants, "the Drawn Sword of Islam."

Twenty-two large galleots belonging to the Turks lay in Algiers. The immediate thought of their leaders was to embark, leave the city, and make their way further east. Not only was there a large Spanish force established at Tlemcen—possibly already on its way to attack them—but news of Aruj's death had put heart into the Algerians, and there could be no doubt that they would try to compound an alliance with the Spaniards. The fort on the island was still in the hands of its Spanish garrison, and the Turks fully expected that they might soon find part of

Charles V's fleet investing the harbour. The obvious course was to escape while the going was good, but wiser counsels prevailed. Their ships were ready, the slaves and stores were embarked, they could leave at an hour's notice—better then, perhaps, to wait a little and see what the Marquis of Comares intended to do.

The latter now made a blunder so gross that it still seems almost unbelievable: "Having settled all his affairs at Tlemcen, [he] withdrew all his Spaniards to Oran, and soon shipped away, for Spain, all except his own proper garrison . . ." Presumably the Marquis felt that in routing Aruj's troops and killing the Turkish leader, he had eliminated all the troublesome elements in that part of North Africa. But, by his failure to follow up his victory and drive the Turks once and for all out of the Algerian coastline, he missed an opportunity which, as Morgan remarked as late as the eighteenth century, "it is very unlikely will ever again offer."

The news was not slow to reach Kheir-ed-Din in Algiers. He heaved a sigh of relief and looked round to see what needed to be done to secure his harbours, towns, and lands. Kheir-ed-Din Barbarossa now "reinforced his garrisons along the coast, at Meliana, Shershell, Tenez, and Mustaghanim, and struck up alliances with the great Arab tribes of the interior." At the same time it seems almost certain that he confirmed his position with the Sultan in Constantinople.

Kheir-ed-Din "got a galleot instantly fitted out for Constantinople, with a letter for his Ottoman Highness, accompanied with rich presents for that monarch, and his chief ministers and favourites; all this he entrusted to the care and direction of his Lieutenant, a faithful and prudent person . . . The purport of the letter and message was to inform the Grand Signor of the situation of affairs in those parts of Africa, to interest his assistance, favour and protection . . ."

The probability is that Kheir-ed-Din did indeed send a ship off to the Sultan. His brother and he had already been in communication with the Sublime Porte—and what more natural than that the survivor should write to the Sultan to acquaint him with Aruj's death? Aruj had become ruler of a large section of North Africa, and it could hardly be considered of little importance to the Ottoman Empire as to who was now the master of that territory. Selim I, who died in 1520, was engaged in conquering Syria and Egypt. It was certainly to his advantage to have these fellow Turks on his left flank holding down Algeria, as well as occupying all the attention of the Spanish monarch. "Bigoted, bloodthirsty, and relentless," as Selim has been called, he was also a conspicuous example of those Turkish rulers who have "understood their trade."

At any rate, from this time onward, Barbarossa was officially accepted by the Sultan as Beylerbey, or Governor-General, of Algiers. This meant that, for the first time, the occupation of this section of the North African coast was an accepted fact by the Sublime Porte. In the career of Kheir-ed-Din Barbarossa this is as important a moment as when Queen Elizabeth I officially acknowledged Francis Drake by knighting him in 1581 aboard the *Golden Hind*.

In 1519, the first year of Kheir-ed-Din's rule of Algiers, he and his men were put to a severe test—one that they had earlier feared would come from the land forces of the Marquis of Comares. The King of Spain realised the error of the previous year, and decided to have done once and for all with the Turkish threat on the North African coast. He intended to eliminate this danger to his sea communications with Naples and Sicily, reinstate garrisons at all the major North African ports, drive out the Turks, restore the original Moslem rulers, and establish satisfactory peace treaties and trading agreements with them. The ruler of Tlemcen and the exiled prince of Tenez were approached, and agreed to give their support if the Spaniards would strike at the heart of the infection—the Turkish forces stationed under Barbarossa in Algiers.

Throughout the spring and early summer the galleys passed and repassed across the Mediterranean Sea, carrying messages between one ruler and another, for this operation was seen as something so important that it transcended national quarrels. Only France, a country which "led an uneasy life with most of its Christian neighbours," does not seem to have contributed to a naval force that amounted to little less than a European armada. Although estimates of the number of ships vary considerably, it would seem that there were about fifty war galleys to spearhead the attack, while the number of transports varies from anything between 200 and 450. Among those who contributed galleys to the fleet were the Knights of St. John, the Pope, the Kingdom of Naples, Monaco, and Spain, while Fernando de Gonzaga and Andrea Doria brought their own fleets, seven galleys in the case of Gonzaga, and fourteen galleys from Genoa under Doria. This, then, was no raid, no simple replenishment of the Spanish garrison on the island of Algiers, but a deliberate attempt to drive the Turks out of North Africa.

Unfortunately, as was so often the case in those days (and indeed it is far from unknown in modern military and naval planning), the organisation of so large an enterprise took a great deal longer than the planners had anticipated. High midsummer, when the great bay of Algiers burns under the eye of the sun and when little more than land and sea breezes distract the surface of the water, would have been the ideal time to launch the attack. The great galleys could have swaggered down easily from the embarkation port of Barcelona, while the transports could have inched their way southwards over a placid sea. But the weeks went by, and still there were delays. German and Italian troops had not yet arrived; galleys were held up by accidents or by the

slowness of dockyards; and Spanish cavalry had to be withdrawn from Sicily, transported across the Mediterranean, disembarked for recuperation, and then re-embarked again. The mus-
tering of an army and the transport of men, munitions, and
cavalry by galleys and slow sailing vessels were among the main
problems of military commanders in those days.

All this activity in the Mediterranean, and on the coast and in
the seaports of Spain, could hardly have gone unnoticed by
Kheir-ed-Din. Both he and his Turkish lieutenants recognised
that if they had escaped attack the previous year, they must certainly be prepared for it in the near future. The money which
had been extracted from the unwilling chief citizens of Algiers
was spent on arms and ammunition and on reinforcing the city's
defences. Throughout the long summer the galley slaves, re-
lieved from their duties at the oar (for no expeditions were
planned for this year), toiled under the harsh sun constructing
walls and building that fortress which Kheir-ed-Din had decided
would one day dominate not only the Bay of Algiers but the
townsfolk themselves. He had also decided in view of the naval
forces being prepared against him that this was certainly no
time to risk a naval engagement. His galleots were excellent for
their task, but as unsuitable against large war galleys as destroyers would be against heavy cruisers. Some were sent away to
Djerba, others scattered up and down the coast in friendly ports
like Djidjelli, while only a limited number were kept beached
outside Algiers to provide an escape route for the Turks if
things went against them.

Although there is no evidence to show that such was the case,
yet there is a possibility that Kheir-ed-Din had received from the
Sultan not only a recognition of his overlordship of the Algerian
coastline, but also some military assistance. This may have been
no more than a token force of janissaries, sent to show that
Selim regarded the Beylerbey of Algiers as worthy of a ruler's

escort. Both Morgan and Lane-Poole have it that "the Sultan sent a guard of two thousand Janissaries to his viceroy's aid, and offered special inducements to such of his subjects as would pass westwards to Algiers and help to strengthen the Corsair's authority . . ." To judge from the Turkish reaction to the threat to their city, one may indeed believe that they had received substantial reinforcements. The year before, when threatened by a far smaller force under the Marquis of Comares, they had seriously considered abandoning the city. Yet this year, when threatened by the full might of Spain and by the sea power of Genoa as well as other Christian powers, there seems to have been no question but that the Turks willingly accepted the prospect of a siege.

The summer was nearly gone when "His Catholic Majesty . . . sent the Armada expressly to drive the Turks from that country; which he presumed might easily be effected since the defeat and death of the Arch-Corsair Barbarossa." Unfortunately for the King and for his troops, ships, and seamen, a greater leader than the first Barbarossa confronted them. But the greatest enemy of all was to prove the weather, which on the Algerian coastline is always a potential enemy to ships and sailors once the summer calm has broken.

Warning the modern navigator about this treacherous part of the sea, the *Admiralty Pilot* writes: "Off the coast of Algeria, the winds set in from westward, as a rule, increasing to gale force with the passage of the cold front of the depression and the accompanying shift to north-westerly or north-north-westerly; in these parts, the gales are frequently preceded by a heavy swell from northward, and their onset is accompanied by characteristic cold-front cloud and thunderstorms with heavy rain. From time to time, after the gale has moderated, the north-westerly winds back again towards westerly with the approach of secondary cold fronts, and the gale is renewed . . ."

In vain had Admiral Hugo de Moncada and his other captains warned Charles against the weather to be expected so late in the year. In vain had they pleaded with him to postpone the expedition until the following spring.

As the great fleet hove in sight, running down from the northwest into the Bay of Algiers, the native Algerians began to take to their heels. They started hiding their valuables in wells and cisterns, loading their womenfolk and children aboard horses and donkeys, and bringing the life of the city to a standstill. But if they were frightened of the advancing enemy, they were even more frightened of their Turkish ruler and his troops. Kheir-ed-Din did not hesitate to warn all potential refugees and looters that immediate execution would be their fate unless they did exactly as he told them. They were to remain in the city and carry on life as normal. He and his troops would protect them against the Spaniards. Remembering the previous executions, they obeyed.

It was St. Bartholomew's Day, August 24, when the fleet arrived off the harbour of Algiers. The northerly swell lifting under their sterns as they came to anchor should have warned the captains of the ships. Perhaps, indeed, it did, but they had little option other than to obey Charles's commands—land the troops, seize Algiers, and exterminate the Turks. Some of the troops had even got ashore—to be attacked immediately by Barbarossa's men—when the storm broke. The wind came out of the north. The waves, which had been building up all the way from the Gulf of Lions, began to burst in rolling fury as they met the North African shore: the first major obstacle in over four hundred miles of open water. Anchors dragged, cables broke, ships collided, oarports burst under the weight of water, and heavy transports encumbered by the gross windage of their high sterns were flung shorewards by wind and sea. Soon the invasion fleet was scattered up and down the coast. The war galleys

hauled themselves laboriously offshore under the groaning labour of their slaves and the crack of the overseers' whips, but
there was little hope for the galleasses and the sailing ships. The
angry shore claimed them—and the Turks waited around the
foam-fringed rocks and murderous sandbanks to kill and capture, to loot and to destroy.

It was one of the worst disasters in the storm-clouded history
of the North African coast. Hundreds of men were drowned and
over twenty ships were total wrecks. Others which lurched
ashore were captured by the waiting Turks; their crews and soldiers were seized and sent to the slave quarters. One huge carrack, we learn, was "full of soldiers, and officers and . . .
many persons of distinction . . . Her equipage might have
been all saved had they held out until the storm abated, when
the galleys returned to pick up what they could." Kheir-ed-Din,
however, went down in person and sent a flag of truce to them
requesting the surrender of their ship. They agreed to his terms.
But when they disembarked it was only with difficulty that Barbarossa and his Turks prevented them from being killed by the
Moorish cavalry. Morgan quotes an anecdote concerning this
event which has all the true flavour of Kheir-ed-Din's personality. Having saved the Spaniards from the undisciplined fury of
the Moors, he asked them whether they themselves agreed that
"persons of rank and distinction should always stand to their
agreements?" Upon the Spaniards replying that such was certainly the case, he asked them why it was that, after the battle in
which his brother had lost his life, the Turks who had agreed to
submit and lay down their arms had been massacred to a man.
"Why," he asked, "did your General break his word with the
Turks to whom he promised life and liberty and, with all their
baggage, free leave to go where they pleased, and yet they were
all killed?"

"By Arabs, My Lord," they replied, "but not by Spaniards."

"So would my Moors infallibly have served every mother's son of you," replied Kheir-ed-Din, "had I not given positive orders to the contrary. But to convince you that I am more a gentleman and man of honour than your faithless General, and mind my word somewhat better, I also promised you life and liberty. The first you actually enjoy; and the other you may, likewise, enjoy whensoever you think fit to purchase it, every one according to his abilities. Whereas all the wealth in Africa would not restore to me one of my slaughtered friends. Let your present servitude and future ransoms make some small atonement for their loss. And from henceforward let this be a warning for every one to have a greater regard to his word of honour."

As a side issue, this anecdote raises an immediate question—in what language did Kheir-ed-Din speak to his Spanish prisoners? We have it on record that he spoke fluent Spanish with a Castilian lisp. Naturally he spoke Turkish; he also spoke Greek, Arabic, French ("well enough to create the belief that he was a native"), and Italian.

The wreck of the fleet, coupled with the considerable loss of life among the troops, was a sad setback to Charles's hopes of exterminating the "Barbary pirates" and clearing his sea lanes. By the following year he was too occupied with events in Europe and with his long-drawn struggle with Francis I of France to concern himself with North Africa. Admiral Hugo de Moncada, meanwhile, had scudded northward with his depleted and damaged fleet to winter in Ibiza.

Kheir-ed-Din, contemplating the plunder and the wrecked shipping and the new slaves in the slave market could afford the luxury of a smile. He did not rest easy on his laurels, however, but continued to work on the defences of his city. In the spring he would summon in the galleys and galleots from their winter refits. The crescent flag of the Sublime Porte would shake above his ships along the coastlines of Christendom. The Kingdom of

Algiers was now established. Soon Kheir-ed-Din would make himself master of the sea and, ultimately, High Admiral of the Ottoman Empire. With his base secured behind him, he would display that genius for naval warfare which entitles him to a high place among the great commanders of all time.

9

KHEIR-ED-DIN
THE SEAMAN

"Kheir-ed-Din, notwithstanding his being Sovereign, as it were, of so many States, never failed, once, or oftener in a year, going out on a cruise with his galleots . . ." It was upon this powerful platform of plunder that Kheir-ed-Din Barbarossa would consolidate his gains and finally ensure that the kingdom founded by his brother would endure for centuries. But, whereas Aruj had been primarily a fighting man, his younger brother was first and foremost a seaman, and—unusual for a sailor—a statesman.

His sea life is incomprehensible without some understanding of the world in which he lived. Like his great rival, Andrea Doria of Venice, he was a soldier as well as a sailor (the close-cut distinction between the one and the other did not really evolve until the eighteenth century). It was, however, as a seaman that Kheir-ed-Din Barbarossa made his mark upon the world. It was as a captain, or rais, of galleys and later as an admiral in charge of them that he transformed the Mediterranean.

"There was always a total difference," wrote Admiral Jurien de la Gravière, "between the Navy of sail and the Navy of the oared galley. There is nothing in common between these vessels."

In fact, there was an almost totally uninterrupted tradition between the galleys of ancient Greece and those of Louis XIV of France. Certainly in the sixteenth century the methods of manouvre, the conditions of life, and the tactics of warfare had changed very little. Navigation methods had definitely improved; so also had the "weight-for-power" ratio of the galleys. No longer were they the complicated two-, three-, or even four-deckers of the classical world.

The sixteenth-century galley was rowed by a crew of men who were all lodged on one deck, with up to six or seven of them handling the loom of the long oar. This technical achievement was comparatively simple, and was based on the same principle as the outrigger that supports the oar of a modern "eight." As Torr comments in *Ancient Ships:* "The single bank of the galley was as effective as the numerous banks of the ancient oar-ships. One of these new systems increased the number of oars by placing them at shorter intervals along the bank, and making them of several different lengths inboard, the rowers being arranged in several lines along the deck: while the other maintained the number of oars at fifty or sixty, but increased their size and strength, several rowers working at every oar."

The term galley derives from the Greek. It is first found in its current interpretation in a treatise attributed to the Emperor Leo VI of Byzantium, to denote warships with a single bank of oars. The great distinction between the galley and the galleon was that the former was primarily an oared vessel, whereas the galleon was a sailing ship only. In between these two came the galleasse, which was both oar- and sail-propelled. In the smaller tonnage class came the galleot, so favoured by the Turks, which was an oared vessel with auxiliary sails but usually with no more than three men to an oar.

In terms which the modern yachtsman can understand: the

galleot was a fast, light, *powered* vessel; the galleasse a fifty-fifty (50 per cent power and 50 per cent sail); the galleon a large *sailing* vessel; and the galley a large, *powered* ship. These were the four main types which were to be found in the Mediterranean throughout the sixteenth, seventeenth, and eighteenth centuries. The rivalry between them was finally to be decided in favour of the galleon (or, in later British terms, ship of the line). With her greater beam and hold space, she was able to accommodate a power of armament that could blast her opponents out of the water long before they—even with their greater manoeuvrability—could get within range. This was something that was to be proved by Francis Drake at Cadiz in 1587 when he shattered the galleys of Spain inside a sheltered harbour where, according to the theories of the time, his sailing ships should have been at a vast disadvantage.

In somewhat similar style, Kheir-ed-Din Barbarossa recognised that for the type of actions which he would be initiating, the small galley or galleot would prove the most useful vessel. A sailing ship, it was true, was faster *when the wind blew*. But in the long Mediterranean summer, especially in the central area, calms often dominated the sea for days on end. Then again, the deeper draught of the sailing vessel was a distinct drawback in many coves and small harbours. Furthermore, a sailing ship could not be launched at its prey like a dart: a galley could be. At the same time, although he was later compelled to have large slave-driven galleys under his command, the smaller galleot manned by fellow Turks was a far more efficient fighting machine.

The objective of a raider like Barbarossa was, after all, not to sink his opponent but to capture him, together with everything and everybody on board. An action, then, consisted in laying your vessel alongside your opponent and capturing him by boarding. It was clearly advantageous to have rowers who, the moment ship was laid against ship, could down oars and add to your fighting strength. Quite apart from this, the hardy Turks were admirable material for the task. As one astute judge of "oar flesh" commented: "The Turks are the best for this work, being vigorous, enduring, uncomplaining, and often well-trained (having already been oarsmen in Turkish galleys) . . . The inhabitants of the Barbary Coast [*i.e.* Moors, Berbers, and Arabs] are nowhere near as good as the Turks, being of an awkward and nervous temperament, and inclined to dogged resistance and invincible stubbornness. They are very difficult to manage and cause innumerable troubles. Negro slaves, on the other hand, just waste away. They are soft and indolent, with little resistance to sickness, and at the slightest bit of cold they die like flies . . ." The buyer who knew this useful bit of advice could save a lot of time and money when looking round a slave market. For the slave market, of course, was not something confined to North Africa or the famous bagnio of Constantinople; it was part and parcel of every great Mediterranean seaport. Whereas it was Christians who were for sale in Algiers, Moslems were for sale in Genoa and Venice.

Pantero Pantera, who was captain of the papal galleys, published an invaluable work on the Mediterranean ships of his period in Rome in 1614 in which he provides some interesting information about the size and types of oars used in galleys. Unfortunately there is no known equivalent Turkish work, but since the Turks and the other Moslems largely based their designs on European types, there is no reason to suppose that there was any great deal of difference between them. The oars of a galleot were usually worked by two or three men apiece. On the galley proper the normal crew to each oar loom was four, although sometimes there might be as many as five or six, while on the hybrid galleasse as many as eight or even more might share the same bench at the loom of one oar. By Pantera's time, about half a century later than Barbarossa's, the large galley had begun to supersede the galleot, since the ability of a ship to with-stand the punishment of heavy cannon fire had now become most important. In the smaller Turkish vessels mainly used by Barbarossa, however, it was not unusual to have only two men to the oar, with a reserve of two. Thus the oars could be worked "watch-and-watch," with two fresh men taking over at regular intervals after a sleep and something to eat.

The lateen sails which graced all Mediterranean galleys were Arabic in origin, although it is possible that they had been first adopted by the Arabs in the Red Sea from local or Indian vessels. Certainly this simple sailing rig had been used by Europeans as early as the first decades of the fifteenth century when the Portuguese caravels (which Prince Henry the Navigator sent out to explore west Africa and the Atlantic) were lateen-rigged. The short mast meant that there was little windage aloft, and in bad weather the long lateen yards could easily be sent down and stowed along the centre line of the vessel. Hoisted on a simple block and tackle, the sails were easy to control, and two or three men could handle a large area of canvas. The lateen had other advantages over the square sail of the contemporary sailing vessel in that it could be used to a certain extent for working to windward. Indeed, until the fore-and-aft rig came into general use in the nineteenth century, the lateen was the most efficient type of sail that man had discovered. In a galleot it was also possible to compensate for the "crabbing" effect on a shallow-draughted vessel—or the large amount of leeway that she would otherwise make—by having the oarsmen pull on the leeward side. Until comparatively recently, Sicilian fishing boats, manned by some ten men, were still sailing small versions of the galleot and going down to the Kerkenah banks off North Africa under oars and sail. In that old haunt of the Barbarossas, the island of Djerba, there are still trading and fishing vessels in commission which differ little from the galleots—except that the main emphasis now is on the sails, and only a few oars are shipped to help make harbour in a calm.

Now that Kheir-ed-Din had control of so much of the Algerian coastline and hinterland he had as much wood as was needed for the construction of an efficient fleet. Pine as always was an important wood in ship construction, although it seems that fir was often preferred for war galleys. But pine, cypress, and, when available, cedar were all used in galley building. The long keel timber was usually of pine, and onto this was fastened a "false keel" of almost any soft wood. This was the expandable keel which was renewed every year, since it tended to get torn or damaged every time that the vessel was run up a beach or onto a slipway.

The vessels were carvel-built, that is to say, with one plank sitting flush upon another, and not, as in the north, clinker-built, where the planks overlap from the gunwale downwards. The seams between the planks were caulked with tow and other packing material, and the caulking was then held in with wax or tar. The whole outer planking was protected by a coat of tar or wax, or the two mixed together. Colouring materials were often mixed with the wax when it was being heated, to improve the vessel's appearance. This type of encaustic paint was reasonably resistant to the wind and weather. The Mediterranean has always been a bad place for the teredo worm, which loves to tunnel its way into wood (finally changing an apparently solid piece of timber into nothing more than a hollow honeycomb), and tar was used on the ships' bottoms as a preventative against this. The frames, timbers, and planks were often secured with wooden dowels, although both bronze and iron nails were also used. The strongest part of the oared vessel was the bow, where heavy catheads stood out proud from the ship's side to assist in tearing away the upper works of an enemy when the galley went in to attack. The *rambade,* or fighting foredeck, also needed additional strengthening, since it was here that the bow-chaser cannon were mounted.

Shallow-draughted as she was, this type of vessel needed some built-in stability to ensure her safety in the short and untidy seas that kick up in the Mediterranean at very short notice. The rowers themselves were disposed about her centre of gravity, but she had the windage of her masts to take into consideration, as well as her raised prow and her built-up quarters in the poop. Here the Turks were often more intelligent than their European foes: living rough and sleeping hard, they did not demand such comfortable quarters aft for their officers and leaders as did the gentry of Spain and Italy. Nevertheless, all galleys and even galleots needed some type of ballasting. This was provided by gravel or stone carried in the bilges and held in place by planks slotted into wooden uprights. These planks could be easily moved, and the ballast quickly transferred from one section of the bilges to another. In this way, by moving ballast from forward to aft, the bows could be elevated slightly—something that was important if the vessel was going in to ram—or, alternatively, if conditions of wind and sea demanded it, the bows could similarly be depressed. Inevitably, the hold collected a mass of foul bilge water, and this had to be kept down to a reasonable level either by a chain of men baling with buckets, or by a simple Archimedean screw worked either by a handle or by a geared-in treadmill.

Drinking water was carried in casks or barricoes, or, in the large galleys, in cisterns which were situated down below to act as additional ballast. Primitive though many of the arrangements might seem to a modern eye, it has to be remembered that the sixteenth-century galley was the product of two thousand years of usage and adaptation. Generations of men had built them, generations had toiled in them, and generations had fought and navigated them. No type of vessel in history has served the human race so long, nor has been so completely understood by its sailors as the Mediterranean galley. Its tactical handling, and the over-all strategy of galley warfare, had been evolved from the Greeks and the Romans, the Byzantines and the Venetians, until there was little room left for improvement. Only in one direction did Turks like Aruj and Kheir-ed-Din make some slight change in the use of their vessels, and that was in preferring free men at the oars and light, fast galleots rather than the heavier vessels favoured by most of the European nations.

Between the years 1520 and 1529 Kheir-ed-Din made himself master of nearly all the coast, with the exception of the island fortress of Algiers which still resolutely held out against him. The port of Col, east of Djidjelli near modern Philippeville, fell into his hands, as did the more important harbour and town of Bône. Inland he secured his hold over the country by becoming master of, the town and trading centre of Constantine. It was during these years that the full realisation of what was happening on the North African coast dawned on the naval powers of Europe—and not only those in the Mediterranean. Even northern countries like England found their merchantships attacked and their Mediterranean trade declining. If the initial spur to Europe's transatlantic exploration had been the Turks cutting off the ancient trade routes to India and the East, this was now given a further impetus by the activities of Kheir-ed-Din and the other captains who swarmed to join his flag on the Algerian coast.

Although he was writing at a later date, the picture that Abbot Diego de Haedo painted of the situation in the Mediterranean gives a good idea of what effect Barbarossa and his companions had upon the trade and the life of this sea: "While the Christians with their galleys are at repose, sounding their trum-

pets in the harbours, and very much at their ease regaling themselves, passing the day and night in banqueting, cards, and dice,
the Corsairs at pleasure are traversing the east and west seas,
without the least fear or apprehension, as free and absolute sovereigns thereof. Nay, they roam them up and down no otherwise
than do such as go in chase of hares for their diversion. They
here snap up a ship laden with gold and silver from India, and
there another richly fraught from Flanders; now they make prize
of a vessel from England, then of another from Portugal. Here
they board and lead away one from Venice, then one from Sicily, and a little further on they swoop down upon others from
Naples, Livorno, or Genoa, all of them abundantly crammed
with great and wonderful riches. And at other times carrying
with them as guides renegadoes (of which there are in Algiers
vast numbers of all Christian nations, nay, the generality of the
Corsairs are no other than renegadoes, and all of them exceed-
ingly well acquainted with coasts of Christendom, and even with
the land), they very deliberately, even at noon-day, or indeed
just when they please, leap ashore, and walk on without the least
dread, and advance into the country, ten, twelve, or fifteen
leagues or more; and the poor Christians, thinking themselves
secure, are surprised unawares; many towns, villages and farms
sacked; and infinite numbers of souls, men, women, children,
and infants at the breast dragged away into a wretched captivity.
With these miserable ruined people, loaded with their own valuable substance, they retreat leisurely, with eyes full of laughter
and content, to their vessels. In this manner, as is too well
known, they have utterly ruined and destroyed Sardinia, Corsica, Sicily, Calabria, the neighbourhoods of Naples, Rome, and
Genoa, all the Balearic Islands, and the whole coast of Spain: in
which last they feast it as they think fit, on account of the Moriscos who inhabit there; who being all more zealous Mohamme-
dans than are the very Moors born in Barbary, they receive and

caress the Corsairs, and give them notice of whatever they desire to be informed of. Insomuch that before these Corsairs have been absent from their abodes much longer than perhaps twenty or thirty days, they return home rich, with their vessels crowded with captives, and ready to sink with wealth; in one instant, and with scarce any trouble, reaping the fruits of all that the avaricious Mexican and greedy Peruvian have been digging from the bowels of the earth with such toil and sweat, and the thirsty merchant with such manifest perils has for so long been scraping together, and has been so many thousand leagues to fetch away, either from the east or west, with inexpressible danger and fatigue. Thus they have crammed most of the houses, the magazines, and all the shops of this Den of Thieves with gold, silver, pearls, amber, spices, drugs, silks, cloths, velvets & c., whereby they have rendered this city [Algiers] the most opulent in the world: insomuch that the Turks call it, not without reason, their India, their Mexico, their Peru."

An interesting point made by Haedo is that so many of the pirate captains who joined their lot with the Turks in North Africa were Christian renegades. Among the outstanding lieutenants of Kheir-ed-Din was Dragut, or Torghoud, a child of Christian parents born in Anatolia and adopted at an early age by a Turkish Governor and converted to Islam. Others were Sinan, a renegade Jew, nicknamed "the Jew of Smyrna," because of his birthplace, and Ochiali, an Italian from Calabria. Records show that in 1588 there were thirty-five galleys and galleots in the fleet of Algiers, twenty-four of them commanded by renegades and only eleven by Turks. Lane-Poole traced the following different nationalities represented among the renegades: "From France, Venice, Genoa, Sicily, Naples, Spain, Greece, Calabria, Corsica, Albania, Hungary, and a Jew." Not all of them, of course, were renegades in the true sense of the term, for some of them were no more than Christian children who had been captured and then trained as Moslems and seamen in Algiers (in rather similar fashion to the janissaries of the Turkish army). The real renegades joined the Moslem forces either because they were fleeing from debt or criminal charges in their own lands, or because they had been captured at sea and had decided to "turn Turk" rather than continue as slaves at the oars. A debtor or a criminal who had been sentenced to a Venetian galley might well feel, if his vessel was overwhelmed and captured by the Turks, that his best course was to throw in his lot with them. Unlike the rich or noble who had every prospect of being ransomed, the poor man had none. He probably had little use in any case for the Christian church. It was no more than sensible to become a convert and enjoy the benefits that this could bring him in a place like Algiers, which was rapidly becoming as rich, prosperous, and civilized as any city in Europe.

In the matter of ship construction there is no doubt that the Turks learned a great deal from their European neighbours. Haedo tells us that "galleys are continually being built and repaired in Algiers" and that "the builders are all Christians, who have a monthly pay from the Treasury of six, eight or ten quarter-dollars, with a daily allowance of three loaves of the same bread with the Turkish soldiery, who have four . . ." Kheir-ed-Din and his richer lieutenants owned their own galleys, but many of those built on the North African coast were often owned by a syndicate. Just as in England, nobles and merchants, even Queen Elizabeth herself, would take shares in the ships to be commanded by Drake and his contemporaries in their raids on Spanish America, so Algerian tradesmen would invest in the building of a galleot or galley. They would appoint their own rais who, in his turn, would be responsible for slaves to row her, and a crew to man and fight her. Unlike the sailors and oarsmen who came under the command of the rais, the troops (janissaries as often as not) came under their own aga. In this respect the

system was not unlike that aboard British and other European
ships of the period, where the soldiery were commanded by their
own officers and had nothing to do with the working of the ship.
At its best this system served to provide a check both upon the
ship's captain and upon the commander of the soldiers. At its
worst it led to the kind of situation that Drake had to resolve on
his voyage round the world, when the military tried to disassoci-
ate themselves from anything to do with the ship. But in the
comparatively short voyages made by Kheir-ed-Din and his fellows such rivalry was less likely to occur, and the fact that the
whole object of the voyage was plunder made both sides of the
ship's company eager to co-operate.

Any idea that because these Turks, renegades, or Moors were
engaged in piracy their ships were badly maintained must immediately be dismissed. Indeed, to quote again from Abbot Haedo:
"their galleots are so extremely light and nimble, and in such
excellent order . . . whereas, on the contrary, the Christian
galleys are so heavy, so embarrassed, and in such bad order and
confusion, that it is utterly in vain to think of giving them chase,
or of preventing them from going and coming, and doing just as
they themselves please. This is the occasion that, when at any
time the Christian galleys chase them, their custom is, by way of
game and sneer, to point to their fresh-tallowed poops, as they
glide along like fishes before them, all one as if they showed
them their backs to salute."

He also goes on to describe how the various groups of galleys
were stationed up and down the coast, some working from the
ports west of Algiers, and others swooping upon the traffic passing south of Sicily from their lairs in Tunis and Djerba. Many of
these raiders, of course, had no connection with Barbarossa but
were acting on their own account, and had made their own private agreements with local Sultans (at Tunis, for instance) just
as Aruj and Khizr had done in their early days. But it was only

the fact that the strong central block of the Algerian coast had come into Turkish hands that gave these other corsairs their freedom to operate with little fear of reprisals.

Among the many summer hideouts of the Turks were the islands of Pantelleria, Linosa, and Lampedusa off North Africa, lying athwart the strait of Sicily. But, so secure had these waters now become for the raiders, they thought nothing of using the coves, harbours, and islands that lay well within Spanish or Italian territory. The superb natural harbour of Bonifacio was another one of their haunts—appropriately enough, perhaps, since it had been the home of the man-eating Laestrygonians, who had destroyed all but one of the ships in Ulysses' squadron when the hero was attempting to find his way home after the Trojan War. Other haunts of the pirates, as Haedo tells us, were "the islands Lipari and Stromboli, near Sicily and Calabria; and there, what with the conveniency of those commodious ports and harbours, and the fine springs and fountains of water, with the plenty of wood for fuel they meet with, added to the careless negligence of the Christian galleys, who scarce think it their business to seek for them—they there, very much at their ease, regale themselves, with stretched-out legs, waiting to intercept the paces of Christian ships, which come there and deliver themselves into their clutches."

It is difficult to imagine these gracious islands, with their vines and white villas (now the haunt of holidaymakers and skin divers), as having been one of the main bases of Barbarossa's terrible Turks. But they certainly chose well. All the traffic bound north and south through the Strait of Messina passes within sight of a watcher on any of the lofty peaks, while the western islands of the group, Alicudi and Filicudi, command the trade route between Naples and Palermo. A corsair's life was not all "battle, murder, and sudden death." There were consolations no doubt in the excellent wine from the slopes of Mount Salvatore and the firm-breasted, dark-eyed girls of Lipari.

10

A YEAR
TO REMEMBER

In 1529 Kheir-ed-Din was engaged in tricky negotiations with the mountain Zouaves, who had shown as little liking for the Turks as they had for any of the other coastal occupiers of the country. The pacification of his territory and the job of welding it into one entity—so that ultimately the whole area would be united under the Turks and against the Spaniards—were exercises in which he showed a greater flair for politics than his brother. Aruj's reaction to difficulties or opposition from neighbours was to go out and "smite them hip and thigh." This simple technique often worked, but it was hardly suitable for holding a country together for any length of time. Kheir-ed-Din was more successful, and by playing upon the fears and distrusts of various local leaders, he seems to have consolidated a large part of the Algerian hinterland behind him. Meanwhile, he was not idle in other directions.

As soon as the summer settled over the sea, he sent out a large raiding party under the command of one of his most able lieutenants, Aydin Rais. With him, as second in command, went Salah Rais, an outstanding sea captain who was later to be described by a French commentator as a man of "noble courtesy";

he was also a most efficient commander of land forces. Aydin Rais, for his part, was one of the most able Turkish seamen afloat, and his reputation among his Christian enemies was almost equal to that of Barbarossa.

Taking fourteen galleots under their command, these two set out under their leader's orders to ransack the Balearic Islands, about 120 miles due north of Algiers. The Balearics, then as now, were rich and fertile, well inhabited, with a number of good harbours. They were an ideal target for a raid, especially when it was known that most of the Spanish fleet was away, taking Charles V to Genoa where he was to be crowned Emperor by Pope Clement VII at Bologna in the following year. Fanning out across the blue acres, the squadron loitered in the channel between the North African coast and the islands. Soon enough a number of merchantmen, some bound from Spain for Naples and Sicily, and others from Italy heading for Spain and the Atlantic, fell into their net.

Moving northwards the galleots now initiated a series of raids on the islands as well as in the Gulf of Valencia. Although they were operating in the home waters of Catholic Spain, the richest and most powerful country of Europe, there was no naval opposition. The western Mediterranean, like the eastern, was in the course of being almost entirely taken over by Moslem Turks. An "abundance of Christians," we learn, were captured during this expedition, and no doubt most of them were sent back straightway in the captured ships to the slave market in Algiers.

The procedure adopted in the slave markets of North Africa, and particularly in Algiers, has been described by Father Dan, a seventeenth-century French priest who wrote a *History of Barbary and the Corsairs*. Although he was writing a century or more after Barbarossa, and although he was engaged in a deliberate work of propaganda designed to arouse the conscience of Christian Europe, there can be little doubt that things had not greatly changed. Indeed, they merely followed the pattern of slave markets that had been in operation in the Mediterranean since the Roman Empire. Lane-Poole paraphrases him: "When they were landed they were driven to the Besistan or slave-market, where they were put up to auction like the cattle which were also sold there; walked up and down by the auctioneer to show off their paces; and beaten if they were lazy or weary or seemed to sham. The purchasers were often speculators who intended to sell again, 'bought for the rise', in fact; and 'Christians are cheap today' was a business quotation, just as though they had been stocks and shares. The prettiest women were generally shipped to Constantinople for the Sultan's choice; the rest were heavily chained and cast into vile dungeons till their work was allotted them, or in the large prisons or bagnios . . . Every rank and quality of both sexes might be seen in these wretched dens, gentle and simple, priest and laic, merchant and artisan, lady and peasant girl, some hopeful of ransom, others despairing ever to be free again."

It was always, of course, more profitable to secure a good ransom from those whose families could afford it, since ransoms were fixed at a price very far in excess of the slave's market value. But for the majority of captives—sailors, soldiers, working men and women on passage between one country and another—there was no hope of ever seeing their homes again. Miguel de Cervantes, author of *Don Quixote,* who was captured in 1575 when returning from Naples to Spain, spent five years in captivity before he was finally ransomed. The rich and powerful might expect to be set free within a few months: provided of course that their relatives were eager to see them again, which was not always the case. Men like Cervantes whose families had a little money might eventually go free, but for the majority it would be work in the fields, in the stone quarries, or in the galleys, until death released them. The prices of slaves fluctu-

ated, of course, like any other market commodity. One seventeenth-century account states that, at that time, a good healthy
slave was fetching five hundred pounds. But when there was a
glut—as after Aydin's successful sortie—fifty pounds or even
less would be a standard price. Even so, the treatment of slaves
was not quite as bad as propagandists like Father Dan tended to
suggest; unless, that is, they were recalcitrant or rebellious.
After all, a slave, like a horse, represented a considerable capital
investment.

Having sent back his captured ships under the control of skel-
eton crews of Turks, Aydin Rais led his galleots on a further
sweep through the Gulf of Valencia, hoping no doubt to pick up
some traffic between Barcelona and southern Spain. It was while
he was in this area that he learned of a number of Morisco families who were vassals on the estate of the Count de Oliva, an
important Valencian nobleman. They begged to be taken over to
North Africa "to live undisturbed in the Religion of their ances-
tors," saying that they were perfectly prepared to pay for their
transport. Aydin Rais accordingly gathered them in from the
nearby country and had them distributed throughout his ships.
Being now somewhat overloaded (for a galleot had little enough
space even for her own crew), he withdrew the squadron to the
small rocky island of Formentera lying due south of Ibiza.

Formentera, smallest and southernmost of the Balearic Islands, was a favourite hideout for the Algerian raiders when
working the western Mediterranean. On its southern side a great
curving bay, backed by sand dunes and pine trees, provided excellent shelter if ever the mistral blew from the Gulf of Lions.
There was adequate water for the ships, and from the main peak
of the island it was easy to keep watch over traffic passing
through the strait between Ibiza and Mallorca. On this occasion
it would seem that the Turks had only recently arrived and had
not had time to set up lookout posts, for they were very nearly

trapped. Eight large Spanish galleys, returning from convoying Charles V to Genoa, were on their way between Barcelona and Valencia when the indignant Count de Oliva sent a message to them saying that his Moriscos had been taken away by the Turks. He also informed General Portundo, the officer commanding the galleys, that sighting reports had indicated the enemy had made for Formentera.

Apparently Aydin and his men had also carried off a great quantity of cash and jewels from the Count's estate, as well as the Moriscos. It was this above all that induced the Count to promise Portundo a personal gift of ten thousand ducats if he would restore his escaped Moriscos and his valuables. Nothing loath, the General turned his ships aside and bore away eastwards towards Formentera. Here was an excellent opportunity of making some money for himself, inflicting a sound thrashing on these insolent Barbary corsairs, and gaining considerable favour with his sovereign.

The four leading galleys of Portundo's squadron were rapidly closing Formentera before they were sighted by the Turks. Aydin was in an awkward position. His galleots, no doubt, were either beached or lying with anchors out ahead and their sterns secured to the shore, as is the normal custom in the Mediterranean. True, he had fourteen galleots, but these were—in theory at any rate—no match for eight large galleys, manned by trained gunners and soldiers and having cannon that could far outrange the light bow chasers of a galleot. Two things he did not know, and could not indeed find out until the action was over. One was that most of the soldiers who would normally have been manning the galleys had been left behind in Italy to take part in Charles's forthcoming coronation; the other was that General Portundo had given strict orders that the galleots were not to be sunk by cannon fire. They were either to be frightened into surrender or captured by boarding. If the General was to get his reward from Count de Oliva, he had to ensure that the Count's valuables were returned intact, as well as his escaped Moriscos. Greed caused his downfall.

Aydin's first reaction was to land the Moriscos immediately. If he had to fight an action, he had no room aboard his galleots for unarmed men, women, and children. He then warped his ships off the beach and moved his galleots under oars out into the bay. He knew that they had no chance of running for it, for a galley was much faster than a galleot. Of course, if he had split up his squadron, some of them might certainly have got away. Possibly he was considering this, when something about the behaviour of the four leading galleys made him pause. These galleys were under the command of General Portundo's son, who had been expressly ordered not to engage by gunfire, but to wait until his father and the other four galleys came up. Young Portundo, therefore, as soon as he was within range of the galleots, instead of opening fire, merely gave orders for the galleys to rest on their oars. General Portundo clearly believed that the sight of eight galleys of Spain would be sufficient to frighten these corsairs into surrender. He did not know his Turks.

Aydin came to the rapid conclusion that what was wrong with these Christians was plain cowardice. Theoretically, most of his squadron should by now have been crippled or sunk by gunfire, while any that might have managed to sneak away should have been pursued and overtaken. Yet nothing happened. He sent his left wing round to the south of the Spaniards, while his right wing drew round in a curve to the north. Then "rowing with the utmost fury, they swooped upon them like eagles, and had surrounded the eight galleys before the amazed Spaniards well knew what they were about."

At this point, if the galleys had had their normal complement of soldiers and arquebusiers, they should have shot the Turks to pieces before they ever managed to get aboard. This was a risk that Aydin must have calculated before making his attack but, perhaps because he had convinced himself that the Spaniards were cowards, he did not hesitate. This moment, when the attack began, was the critical climax to all galley actions.

"At last we drew near to her side under the full power of our oars, giving out the 'chamade', which is the loud shouting noise that the rowers make to frighten the enemy. And it is a really terrifying thing to see three hundred men, on board each galley, naked as Adam, shouting all together and rattling their chains— the sound of which adds to their cries and makes anyone tremble who is unaccustomed to it . . ." These are the words of a slave who served aboard a Christian galley, but they were just as applicable to a Turkish vessel. Indeed, the high war cry of the rowers as they came in for the final assault had been part and parcel of the Mediterranean world since the galleys of Athens. So, now, the Turks at their oars were shouting "Allahu-Akbar! Aaaallah!" as the first shots were exchanged between the arquebusiers.

By encircling the Spanish galleys, Aydin Rais had ensured that his own forward guns—light though they were—were brought to bear upon the long, oared flanks of the enemy. The Spaniards by failing to open fire from their bow chasers in the early stages had entirely lost their advantage. (Galleys, like galleots, had no side armament and could therefore only use their cannon when they had the enemy ahead of them.) It is difficult at this remove of time to visualize that moment on the hot sultry sea when the swords were unsheathed, the muskets fired, the bow cannon boomed, and the oars churned the water into quick eyes of foam.

Kipling with the intuition of genius caught something of it: "Then we closed up on the other ship, and all their fighting men jumped over our bulwarks, and my bench broke and I was pinned down with the other three fellows on top of me, and the big oar jammed across our backs . . . I could hear the water sizzle, and we spun round like a cockchafer and I knew, lying where I was, that there was a galley coming up bow-on, to ram us on the left side. I could just lift up my head and see her sail over the bulwarks. We wanted to meet her bow to bow, but it was too late. We could only turn a little bit because the galley on our right had hooked herself on to us and stopped our moving . . . Then her nose caught us nearly in the middle, and we tilted sideways, and the fellows in the right-hand galley un-hitched their hooks and ropes, and threw things on to our upper deck—arrows, and hot pitch or something that stung, and we went up and up and up on the left side, and the right side dipped, and I twisted my head round and saw the water stand still as it topped the right bulwarks, and then it curled over and crashed down on the whole lot of us . . . It looked like a silver wire laid down along the bulwarks, and I thought it was never going to break."

That was a galley action—that, and the long splintering sound as the oars broke under the impetus of the charging beak of the enemy. That—and the screams of the rowers as the looms of the oars chopped back into their chests and faces and killed them.

Aydin Rais aided by another galleot had made straight for the Captain-Galley, the flagship of Spain, aboard which the dumb-founded General Portundo watched the ruin of his hopes and of his squadron. Both Turkish galleots, coming in on opposite sides, smashed their prows into the flagship. Their boarding par-ties leaped over the bulwarks and made straight for the poop where the General and his staff had drawn their swords and stood waiting. In the melee that followed, a Turkish arquebusier managed to shoot Portundo in the chest. The wound was mortal; panic spread through the Spaniards; the flagship surrendered. This was not the beginning of the end, but the end itself. All around, the quick and eager galleots were carrying their encumbered foes—encumbered by the size of their ships and by the fact that the soldiers who should have been manning them were absent.

Only one galley, the crack of the whip sounding over the rowers' backs, turned away in the confusion and managed to escape. Hotly pursued by some of the galleots, she made her way to Ibiza. She found safety at Salina, that cape where the flat white salt pans blaze under the sun. The other seven galleys of Spain surrendered one after another. The whole action was a perfect example of the fact that it is not the size and weight of armament that necessarily wins battles, but efficient armament efficiently handled. Morale was then—as it is still—the prime requisite for success.

Almost unbelievably, Aydin Rais, Salah Rais, and their Turks, had turned what should have been a certain defeat into an incredible victory. They released their fellow countrymen and coreligionists from their chains, and then turned back into the long sandy bay of Formentera to collect their Morisco passengers. The latter, who had been nervously watching the whole action, prepared to flee towards the heights of the island if the Spaniards had won, came down and were re-embarked. Aydin and his lieutenants now spent several days in the anchorage, making their arrangements for the officering of the captured ships, for the distribution of passengers, and for the immediate repair of planks, oars, and rigging that had been damaged in the action.

It was an astounding action. British histories, for instance, which make much of the successes of Francis Drake against the Spaniards (such as his capture of the great *San Felipe* off the Azores in 1587) never mention the day when a captain of Barbarossa's fleet took on eight large war galleys of Spain in an engagement which, by all the rules of war, should have gone the other way, and defeated them.

But then whoever—in any country in the world—has history truly presented to him? The English try to be objective, but are far from successful. The Spaniards have considerable honesty, but a strong religious bias. The Italians use their charm like a smoke screen. The French (so soon after this particular episode to become allied with the Turks) merely lie. The Americans and the Russians often pretend that any history prior to their own is somewhat irrelevant. But the history of the Mediterranean is important, because the whole of Western culture stems from this sea and the land surrounding it. To see the culture and the technical achievements of the Mediterranean basin as totally European is as stupid as maintaining that there is positive in electricity but no negative. The whole story of the cultures that have arisen in this part of the world stems from the fact that it is here that the interrelation between East and West is most acutely felt.

Aydin Rais and Salah Rais returned to Algiers, and to a most deserved triumph. Behind them they had in tow, or under their command, seven of Spain's great galleys and, among them, the flagship of the Spanish Mediterranean fleet. General Portundo, the commander of the squadron, had been killed, but his son was among the prisoners—together with six other noble captains. Scions of many of the most highly connected families in Spain were among the captives (all of them certain for valuable ransoms), and hundreds of Christians could soon be offered for sale. As an additional bonus, Aydin and his men had freed a number of Moriscos, all eager to become good citizens of Algeria. They had captured a large quantity of marketable treasure and had freed dozens of Moslems from the oar benches of the Spaniards. Fifteen twenty-nine was a year to remember.

11

BARBAROSSA ENTERS THE GOLDEN HORN

Kheir-ed-Din is described by one commentator as "having en-
vied his old crony the honour and reputation he had acquired by
having the sole direction of that so-much-talked-of exploit."
This is possible, but Barbarossa was far too intelligent to have
let it be evident, and his relationship with Aydin Rais remained
as friendly as ever. In any case, during the time that the galleots
had been away at sea, Kheir-ed-Din had managed to make useful alliances with the Zouaves and with another local ruler, Beni
Abbas. This was just as important to the new Turkish state of
Algeria as any successes upon the high seas. Barbarossa had
also come to the conclusion that he was now so powerful that he
could no longer tolerate the Spanish garrison on the Peñón of
Algiers. True, it was not important enough to exert any real influence upon the coastline, but it was still a great inconvenience,
preventing him from using the inner port of the harbour for the
security of his galleys. He had long followed his brother's theory
that—given Algiers and local power—he had only to wait until
the right time, and the Spanish fortress would fall like a ripe
plum into his hand. The time was now. The Spaniards were dis-

couraged, and the King of Spain was away being crowned Emperor by the Pope.

Kheir-ed-Din "knew the Spaniards dreaded him almost everywhere and was quite scandalised to find himself driven by them to many incommodities, by a scurvy fort, which they needs would maintain, just in his teeth . . ." The success of Aydin Rais further confirmed him in his opinion that, having reinforced his own city, he could now get rid of the Spaniards without much trouble.

He needed the full advantages of the harbour, especially now that he had so many galleys and galleots under his command. So, in the spring of 1530, he set himself to remove the obdurate Spanish garrison. He had ordered several large siege guns from Constantinople, and had started an armoury of his own in Algiers. In any case, he had sufficient equipment to feel that he could batter the garrison into submission without having to hazard a landing-craft assault upon it—something that might well have cost him a considerable number of his best Turkish troops.

The Governor of the fort was Don Martin de Vargas. He was the type of Spanish nobleman who has gone down in history as being not only well-born, but also as accepting all the responsibilities which in those days were a requirement for belonging to the privileged classes. *Noblesse oblige* was far from being a meaningless catch phrase. It did, indeed, mean what it said— that, if you were of the nobility you would discharge your obligations according to the high and hard standards that were demanded. Of course, only too often, the well-bred cheated and escaped their responsibilities, but in general—and this was particularly true of the Spaniards—they felt that they would rather die than suffer the shame of not living up to the ideals set for their class. Don Martin's reply to Kheir-ed-Din Barbarossa's offer of safe conduct, if he and his men surrendered, was classic: "I am astonished to hear a person of such worth, and so good a soldier as the Pasha of Algiers, making such an inglorious and

Kheir-ed-Din Barbarossa

HORUSCE und HAREADEN BARBAROSSA
Könige von Tunis und Algiers und ober See Admiralen

Aruj and Kheir-ed-Din Barbarossa

A galley running before the wind

A galley at anchor, with awnings supported upon the oars, and with the galley chimney erected

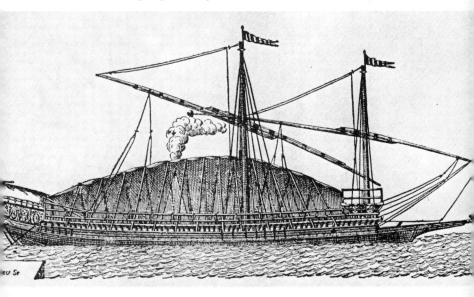

An Admiral's galley

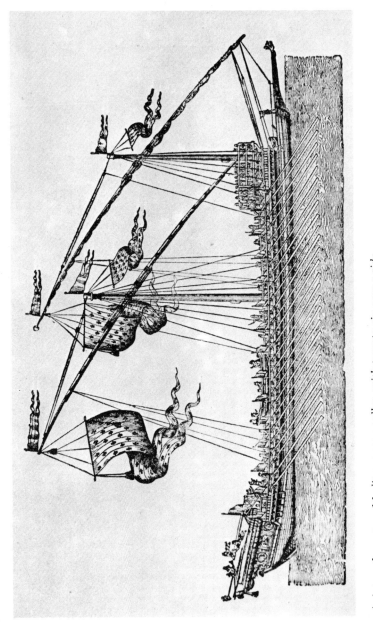

A sixteenth-century Mediterranean galley, with twenty-six oars a side

ANDREAS DE AVRIA

Admiral Andrea Doria

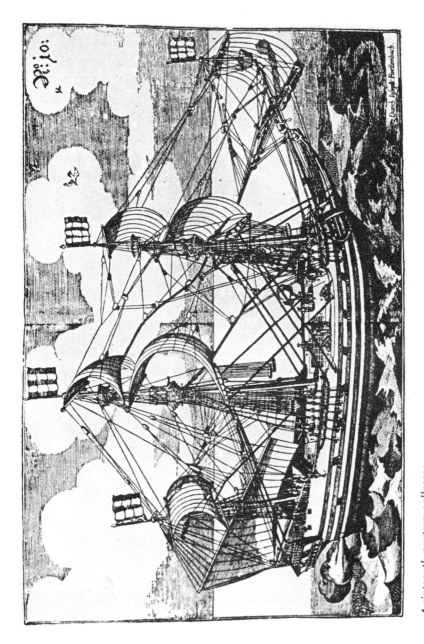

A sixteenth-century galleasse

A galleon of the Knights of Malta

scandalous proposal to one who is of no less worth, and no worse a soldier either. Such a suggestion might be acceptable to people who little value their honour. But I would remind you that you are dealing with Spaniards, in whose breasts your vain and fruitless menaces can cause neither dread, nor any apprehension."

Barbarossa can have had no doubt that this was the reply he would get and, indeed, had all his siege guns ready to open fire as soon as this formality was over. On May 6, 1530, the siege of the Peñón of Algiers was opened. It continued for a full fifteen days, naval guns firing their iron cannon balls at the crumbling walls and a great *murlaccio* hurling huge stone shot from its cavernous mouth. It is a tribute to Spanish courage that the garrison of no more than two hundred men held out for so long in the face of such an implacable assault. Perhaps they hoped for some relief ships from Spain (which were shortly due), but no relief came. On the sixteenth day, the main Turkish attack was launched through a huge breach in the walls. Only fifty-three men and the commander, Martin de Vargas, were found alive. They were sent to the slave quarters to join their fellow Spaniards captured in Aydin's recent raid.

According to one version, Barbarossa offered Don Martin his freedom if he would become a Moslem, adding that, in honour of his courage, he would be happy to appoint him captain of his personal guard. The Spaniard's reply to this suggestion is said to have been so haughty and insulting (referring to the Moslem faith as "a false and ridiculous sect") that Barbarossa had him executed on the spot. But another account states that Don Martin was sent to Shershell along with other important Spanish captives, and was killed there by the Turks for trying to assist the Spaniards during their raid on Shershell in the following year. There is, in fact, no reliable evidence as to the gallant commander's fate.

Barbarossa's first action after the capture of the fort that had so long been a thorn in his side was to order its complete destruction. Then, using stones from the fort and from local quarries, he set all the slaves to work on constructing a breakwater to connect the island to the mainland of Algiers. It was just after this had begun that a number of transports, loaded with men and ammunition for the relief of the Peñón, came sailing unsuspecting down the coast. Barbarossa ordered out the galleots, which swooped like hawks on their prey, capturing (according to De la Gravière) "two thousand seven hundred men and a considerable quantity of arms and provisions." It was an additional triumph and, meanwhile, the Peñón of Algiers was no more. Within two years, a great stone môle protected the harbour of Algiers from northerlies and westerlies, while inside lay an ever-increasing fleet of galleys and galleots—a symbol of the new sea power of North Africa.

The addition of so many sea captains and ships to the growing Moslem strength in the western Mediterranean was largely due to the fact that in recent years there had been practically no Christian naval vessels operating anywhere in the eastern Mediterranean. The last threat to Turkish power in the Aegean and the Levant had been eliminated in 1522 when the Sultan Suleiman had driven the Knights of St. John out of the island of Rhodes, after a siege in which he had lost thousands of men. The expulsion of the knights from Rhodes had been an immense blow to Christendom, for the knights were the finest fighting sailors of their day, and had long been the principal opponents of Ottoman sea power in the east. For seven years they had been homeless; and it was only now, in 1530, that they took up residence in Malta—the island which was to become so indelibly associated with their name that they finally became known throughout Europe not as the Knights of St. John, but as "the Knights of Malta." But all this was in the future, and at the moment the knights—engaged in settling into their new home

114

and extending its primitive fortifications—represented no threat to the Turkish dominance of the Mediterranean.

Bushy-bearded Kheir-ed-Din built well upon the foundations that his brother had laid. Lane-Poole summarised his achievements during this period of his life: "Everything that Kheir-ed-Din took in hand seemed to prosper. His fleet increased month by month, till he had thirty-six of his own galleots perpetually on the cruise in the summer season; his prizes were innumerable, and his forces were increased by the fighting men of the seventy thousand Moriscos whom he rescued in a series of voyages, from servitude in Spain. The waste places of Africa were peopled with the industrious agriculturalists whom the Spanish Government knew not how to employ. The foundries and dockyards of Algiers teemed with busy workmen. Seven thousand Christian slaves laboured at the defensive works and the harbour; and every attempt of the Emperor to rescue them and destroy the pirates was repelled with disastrous loss."

An attack on Shershell in the summer of 1531 by twenty galleys of Spain, although it resulted in some Christian prisoners being released, was repulsed without much difficulty, and Barbarossa was "comforted to learn that near 900 of such impertinent visitors [the Spaniards] had been cut to pieces," and that he had more than six hundred new captives. The commander of this unsuccessful expedition was Andrea Doria. His reverse rankled, and he no doubt looked forward to a further meeting with Barbarossa. Shortly afterwards the latter led out his ships on one of his annual summer raids and captured two Neapolitan galleys on their way with cargoes of silk from Messina to Spain. Later in the year, an attempted rising by the slaves in the bagnio was discovered and suppressed long before it could become dangerous. Barbarossa could undoubtedly call it a good year—the Spaniards repulsed at Shershell, a valuable cargo brought to port, and a weakness in the system exposed and cured.

115

It must be borne in mind that the divided state of Europe played a large part in all the Turkish successes of these years. While Spain and France were at loggerheads, while England was contesting with Spain and Portugal the rights to the new territories across the Atlantic, and while Italy was divided between papal power, egocentric princes, and the Spanish-dominated Kingdoms of Naples and Sicily, there was little hope of any co-ordinated action against the Turks. While Islam united many nations and different ethnic groups under its flag, Christianity seemed to be used merely as a qualification for being a European. After that, there was no need to pretend to "love your neighbour." This was part of the penalty that Christianity had to pay for having become the "national" religion of the Romans and, later, of the Byzantines. Once any chance of union between the Eastern and Western churches had been shattered by the Fourth Crusade in its destruction of the Byzantine Empire, Christianity as a supranational force was bound to collapse. Its place was taken by European nationalism, and it was against this "house divided against itself" that the Kingdom of Algiers and the power of the Barbarossas was enabled to rise. The Turks, according to the Abbot Haedo, "held the Christians in great contempt," and it is not at all difficult to understand the reason for this. As professing Christians, the inhabitants of Europe were, of course, contemptible. They worshipped "graven images"; contrary to their own and the Moslem faith they had superimposed upon the pantheon of the ancient gods innumerable saints and martyrs (many of them bogus); and, while professing to be adherents of the God of Love and Peace, they spent much of their time killing one another.

But while the western as well as the eastern ends of the Mediterranean were now indisputably dominated by the Turks, the situation in the central basin, the Ionian Sea, was not so favourable to the Sultan. In 1532, the year after his repulse at Shershell, Andrea Doria conducted a remarkably successful campaign against the Grecian outposts of the Ottoman Empire. The great Genoese Admiral had withdrawn his allegiance from Francis I of France some four years before, and had taken over his own twelve galleys to join the cause of Charles V. This was an immense blow to France, for the added strength of the imperial navies, combined with the skill of Doria, entirely altered the naval balance of power between the two great rivals. The object of Doria's raid on Greece was to create a diversion and take some of the pressure off Hungary, where the Sultan was advancing into imperial territory at the head of his armies. Doria brilliantly attained his objective, sweeping in through the Gulf of Patras, capturing the city, and going on to seize the two forts which commanded the narrow entrance to the Gulf of Corinth. Prior to his attack on Patras, Doria had captured the important garrison port of Coron commanding the Gulf of Messenia in the southern Peloponnese. In the spring of the following year, hearing that the garrison he had left behind was blockaded by a Turkish fleet, Doria fought an inspired action, defeated Lutfi Pasha in command of the Turkish fleet, and reinforced and revictualled the garrison.

There seems no doubt that it was Doria's successes against the Turkish navy—and in their own home waters—that prompted Sultan Suleiman's next action. His Grand Vizir Ibrahim had long been urging the Sultan to institute closer relations with the new ruler of Algiers. He was eager to cement a friendship between the Sublime Porte and these Turks in the western Mediterranean who had been enjoying such overwhelming success against the forces of Spain and the Emperor. In the spring of 1533 Kheir-ed-Din Barbarossa, Beylerbey of Algiers, received an ambassador from Constantinople. He was commanded to present himself before Suleiman, Sultan of the Ottomans and "Allah's Deputy on Earth," at his earliest convenience. It was a moment of triumph for Barbarossa. Nearly thirty years previously he had left the Aegean as an obscure young man in the service of his brother, with two small galleots. He was now ruler of nearly all Algeria, master of a fleet that terrorised the western Mediterranean, and important enough to have the most powerful ruler on earth requesting his presence at court. For Barbarossa must have realised that the Sultan's need for him in Constantinople was dictated by the fact that he, Barbarossa, had proved himself uniquely successful against the Christians— especially at sea.

"The issues," writes Sir Godfrey Fisher, "which led to Kheir-ed-Din's urgent summons to Constantinople appear to have been threefold—the reorganisation of the Turkish fleet, which had fallen into disrepute; the importunity of a claimant to the throne of Tunis . . . and the opportunity of effecting an arrangement for active co-operation with France in the Mediterranean which had apparently been advocated and, indeed, initiated by Barbarossa himself—perhaps to counteract friendly advances which the emperor was making to the sultan."

Certainly the all-important issue was the reorganisation of the fleet: a necessity which Doria's recent successes had brought home harshly to the Sublime Porte. It had certainly not escaped the notice of the Grand Vizir that, whereas Turkish ships under Turkish admirals commanded little success against the Genoese, Barbarossa and his lieutenants seemed to rule the western Mediterranean as its almost undisputed masters. Whereas Doria's attack on Shershell had been beaten off with heavy losses, he was still able to cruise around the Ionian with the same impunity that Barbarossa enjoyed in the central and western sea. Barbarossa was a self-made man—like the Grand Vizir—and the latter could respect and understand the qualities which had lifted the son of an obscure janissary to power and prominence. Barbarossa was clearly the man to advise on the reorganisation of the navy and, indeed, even on the design of its ships and equipment.

On the second question, the sovereignty of Tunis, there can be no doubt that the initiative came from Kheir-ed-Din. He had carefully left the Tunisian area alone while organising Algeria, but he must no doubt have kept a watchful eye on this Moslem state on his right flank. He had many friends and acquaintances in Tunis, dating from the days when he and his brother had used it as their headquarters. In 1532, prior to the Sultan's summons, he had already received a number of messages from leading citizens in Tunis imploring him to free them from their current ruler, a certain Muley Hassan of the dynasty of Hafs. Muley Hassan was an example of the worst type of North African prince, a man who is said to have stepped to the throne over the bodies of twenty-two (some authorities go so far as to say forty-four) murdered brothers. The Tunisians would doubtless have forgiven this blood-stained path to the throne if their new ruler had been efficient, and sympathetic to the interests of the ruling classes. Muley Hassan was neither.

Barbarossa, no doubt, communicated to the Sultan that there was a prospect of extending Turkish rule throughout Tunisia as well as Algeria. This was almost certainly one of the reasons why he received the imperial summons. Kheir-ed-Din could be useful to the Sultan in reorganising his navy. No doubt the Sultan could be useful to Kheir-ed-Din in providing arms and men for the occupation of Tunis. In either case, both seemed certain to benefit.

The third reason for the Sultan's summons—and one which to Barbarossa was certainly as important as any—was the question of which nation the Turks would back in the internecine struggles of Europe. Overtures had recently been made to the Sultan by Charles V, eager to avert the Turkish threat to his territory in central Europe. He was equally eager to get the Sultan to call off, if he could, the rapacious attacks on his Mediterranean trade routes by Barbarossa and his fellow galley captains. Barbarossa's interests, on the other hand, were best served by a collaboration with France. France had little or no interest in the North African coast, while any alliance that could damage Spanish power was of the greatest advantage to Algiers. It was up to him to persuade the Sultan that the most advantageous alliance for the Ottoman Empire was with France. With the help of France there was a better chance of imposing upon central Europe that extension of his Empire which Suleiman so ardently desired.

"In August 1533, he [Barbarossa] having appointed Hassan Aga Viceroy of Algiers, along with two other lieutenants of his, stopping *en route* to put down trouble in Constantine," left Algeria for the Aegean, the Sea of Marmora, and the Bosphorus. Some records have it that the squadron with which Barbarossa left Algiers inflicted great damage on the territories through which they passed. It seems unlikely, and Hamilton Currey's statement that "sailing through the Straits of Bonifacio they touched Monte Cristo etc." is uncorroborated by any known evidence. It was unlikely that, being bound for Constantinople, Barbarossa would have diverged so far from his route as to go right up into the northern Mediterranean, when all he had to do was to take the straightforward eastern route south of Sicily and Greece, round Cape Matapan up into the Aegean. It does seem, however, from an analysis of the varying accounts, that he netted a number of corn ships bound from Sicily to Spain as his squadron swung easily eastward into the sea that belonged to the Sultan.

Sandoval, Bishop of Pamplona, in his history of the Emperor Charles V, has a good—but possibly imaginative—account of Barbarossa's reception when he and his galleys and galleots rounded Seraglio Point and came into the Golden Horn. They rowed with easy confidence, the galley of Barbarossa distin-

guished from those of his lieutenants by the broad gold line
which indicated the Sultan of several Algerian cities, and the
Pasha and Beylerbey of Algiers. "A concordance of sweet
sounds" was heard far off, for Barbarossa—like Sir Francis
Drake again—was fond of music aboard ship. He had a similar
sense of the respect that should be shown to a man who had
made his way in the world, and who was a master mariner, general, and sea captain. He had brought presents for the Sultan
that established his position, presents such as few men—even
kings—could afford to bring. Camels laden with gold and gems,
silks and bales of rich velvets, were preceded by some two hundred young Christian women (destined for the Sultan's harem),
each of them carrying a gift of gold or silver in her hand. Lions
and other African animals followed. Behind them, riding upon a
bay stallion that the Sultan himself had sent to him as a gift,
came Barbarossa. "The tried generals and statesmen of the
greatest of Ottoman emperors assembled to gaze upon the rough
sea dogs, whose exploits were on the lips of all Europe; and
most of all they scrutinized the vigorous well-knit yet burly
frame of the man with the bushy eyebrows and thick
beard . . ." It is doubtful whether Kheir-ed-Din was overim-
pressed by the packed ranks of janissaries lining his route, or the
splendour of the city through which he was passing. Like all men
who have triumphed through their own endeavours alone, Kheir-
ed-Din rode into Constantinople asserting a dignity that he knew
was unassailable.

12

CREATOR OF
THE OTTOMAN NAVY

During that winter, with the assistance of the Vizir Ibrahim, Barbarossa convinced the Sultan that the division of power in Europe would be best maintained by aiding the French at the expense of the Emperor Charles V. The Sultan's interests lay in expanding his land empire; Barbarossa's in maintaining his sea empire. The natural enemy of the Sultan and the ruler of Algiers was Charles V. But, to aid France against the Emperor, a really efficient fleet was essential: a fleet that could successfully challenge Charles's Admiral, Andrea Doria, on the high seas.

Barbarossa turned his attention first of all to the dockyard of the capital. He soon found that there was general waste and confusion, and that the Turks seemed to know little about ship construction or design. Now Barbarossa and his lieutenants were not only skilled men of the sea, but they had had to learn during their roving years a great deal about ship repair and building. They had also had plenty of experience in battle and had minutely examined innumerable captured ships—galleasses from Spain, galleys of Naples, and large trading carracks. There can have been few seamen anywhere in the Mediterranean, not ex-

cluding admirals like Doria, who had any such comparable
knowledge of everything to do with ships—from their construction to their maintenance and repair, and to the handling of
them in action.

Ibrahim, the Grand Vizir, on his first meeting with Kheir-ed-
Din had quickly discerned his qualities and had had no hesitation in writing to the Sultan: "We have set our hand upon a
veritable man of the sea. Have no hesitation in naming him
Pasha, Member of the Divan, and Captain General of the
Fleet." Reinforced by his official appointment, and by the ap-
proval shown him by both Sultan and Vizir, Barbarossa set to
work to transform the dockyard of the Sublime Porte. Indeed, as
Jean Chesneau, French Secretary at Constantinople, reported in
1543: "The supremacy of Turkey at sea dates from Kheir-ed-
Din's first winter in the dockyards of this city."

There was no shortage of pine, fir, or cypress in the domains of
Turkey; nor were competent carpenters and craftsmen difficult
to find among the Greeks, Bulgarians, Albanians, and other
races in the Ottoman Empire. What had previously been lacking
was a co-ordinating intelligence, coupled with advisers in design
and construction. All these things Barbarossa supplied. To
quote Jean Chesneau again: "Over at Pera [the northern side of
the Golden Horn] there is a shipyard on the shore where they
both build and maintain galleys and other ships. Normally there
are two hundred skilled master-craftsmen working here, who
each earn ten aspers a day, and fifty superintendents earning
twelve aspers a day. Working in the dockyard are a great number of labourers who are paid four aspers a day . . . In charge
of all this there is a Captain-General, whom the Turks call a
Beylerbey of the Sea, who also has charge of the navy when it
goes out. In the past this Beylerbey was always the Commander
of Gallipoli. But after the Grand Turk gave the office to Barbarossa (who received 14,000 ducats a year for the position), this

revenue was drawn out of the islands of Mitylene, Rhodes and Euboea—from which, in fact, he extracted three times as much . . ." It is interesting to note that Barbarossa's salary was derived from the three most important islands in the Aegean at that time, and that his own birthplace, Mitylene, was among the main subscribers.

Chesneau goes on to explain the state of the Turkish navy prior to Barbarossa's reformation: "Before he took charge, the Turks, with the exception of some corsairs, did not know anything about the seaman's art. When they wanted to find the crews for a fleet, they went into the mountains of Greece and Anatolia and brought in the shepherds (whom they call 'gouiounari', that is to say, 'sheep-watchmen') and put them to row in the galleys and to serve aboard the other ships. This was quite hopeless, for they knew neither how to row or be sailors, or even how to stand upright at sea. For this reason the Turks never made any showing at sea. But all at once Barbarossa changed the whole system." Admiral Jurien de la Gravière confirmed this when he commented on the above: "He changed it so much that in a few years they acquired the reputation of being invincible."

Barbarossa was a practical man first and foremost; he was also a man of vast and far-reaching ambition. Unlike Aruj, the brilliant soldier-of-fortune, Kheir-ed-Din was a planner who worked carefully. It is possibly true that, as Ekrem Rechid wrote of him, "he saw the earth, the entire earth with its continents, its seas, its coasts and its vast expanses of desert, and he dreamed of a wonderful empire which could stretch all the way from the East to the West—to the West, beyond the ocean, and the New World. He dreamed of populating the New World with virile men and of planting there his Standard and his Religion. He dreamed of conquering the Indies and of reaching China . . ." This poetic conception of the great Kheir-ed-Din is, perhaps, not so far removed from the truth. Yet it is also true that he pursued his objectives (whatever they may ultimately have been) in a pragmatic fashion. His object in Constantinople was not only to endear himself to the Sultan and to improve the latter's navy, but also to achieve his own ambitions.

Tunis was Barbarossa's main preoccupation at this moment. If he made sure that the dockyard of the Sultan never ceased from work throughout that winter, it was not only that he had the Sultan's welfare at heart. True, he had promised the Sultan the Kingdom of Tunisia (which he, Barbarossa, would rule for him), but he hoped to secure for himself and his successors a kingdom that would stretch from the Strait of Gibraltar to Tripoli. Master of all that was worth having on the North African coast, he would then be in a position to talk with considerable authority at the divan with the Sultan of the Ottomans. Moreover, as master of the ships that gave the Sultan freedom of the Mediterranean (and would one day, perhaps, transport his troops to the mainland of Italy and Spain), he may well have seen how even the all-conquering Sultan might come to regard him as indispensable. "Inspiring his men with his own marvellous energy, he laid out sixty-one galleys during the winter, and was able to take the sea with a fleet of eighty-four vessels in the spring."

Any idea that Turks like Barbarossa, even when it came to the skills of the navigator, were less efficient than their western confreres must be immediately dismissed. The science of navigation had, indeed, been promoted in Moslem countries, and a large part of the European knowledge of the subject came from their contacts over the past two centuries with Moslem sea captains. It is worth noting, for instance, that when Henry the Navigator was beginning his attack on the Atlantic sea routes in the early fifteenth century it was to Mallorcan Jews like Jafuda Cresques that he looked for information. The charts of the Arabs and their knowledge of the west African world and of the

Red Sea and the Indian Ocean were eagerly sought after. Was it not written in the Koran that "It is Allah who hath appointed for you the stars, so as to guide yourselves in the darkness of land and sea. The signs have been made distinct for those people who have been given the knowledge"?

In an Arabic manuscript dated as early as 1282 there is a section that indicates a clear knowledge of the magnetic compass: "Sea-captains of Syria, when the night is dark and they cannot see the stars which show the four cardinal points, take a vessel of water which they shelter from the wind by going below. They take a needle which they thrust into a piece of acacia or a straw so that it forms a cross. They throw it into the water. The captains then take a lodestone of a size to fill the hand or smaller. They bring it towards the surface of the water and make a circular movement from the right with the hand: the needle follows it round. Then they abruptly withdraw it, and the needle turns to stand in the north-south line. This operation I saw myself on a voyage from Tripoli in Syria to Alexandria in 1242–3."

Certainly there can be no doubt that the compass was first introduced into Europe by the Arabs, who, almost certainly, derived their knowledge from the East and from China. Tiraboschi, in support of his theory that the compass was introduced into Europe by the Arabs, mentions the fact that they were superior to Europeans in scientific learning and in navigation. In later centuries, European writers (Sir J. Chardin [1643–1713], for instance) were only too prone to assume that "the Asiatics are beholden to us for this wonderful instrument." Yet, as early as 1498, we gather from a Portuguese description of a chart shown to Vasco da Gama by an Arab that it not only had compass points on it, but that "the coast was laid down with great certainty by these two bearings of North and South, and East and West."

The Arabs, from whom the Turks learned their navigation,

were extremely skilled. As the historian Sismondi remarked: "It is characteristic of the Middle Ages that when all their pretended discoveries are mentioned, they are always spoken of as if they were just in general use. Gunpowder, the compass, Arabic numerals, and paper—none of them are mentioned as new and original discoveries. Yet they must have effected a complete change in war, navigation, science, and education."

It is certain that Barbarossa and his lieutenants had a great deal to teach the Turkish shipmasters in navigation, as much as anything else. Whereas the latter had been almost entirely engaged in the island-studded Aegean, the others had had to confront the long silent seas north of Africa and the reaches between Algiers, Gibraltar, and beyond. A German monk, Felix Faber, on a voyage to the Holy Land in 1483 gave an interesting picture of the navigational methods in current use aboard a merchantman: "Besides the pilot, there were other learned men, astrologers and watchers of omens who considered the signs of the stars and sky, judged the winds and gave directions to the pilot himself. And they were all of them expert in the art of judging from the sky whether the weather would be stormy or tranquil, taking into account besides such signs as the colour of the sea, the movements of dolphins and of fish, the smoke from the fire, and the scintillations when the oars were dipped into the water. At night they knew the time by an inspection of the stars . . ." The monk's description is interesting, for apart from the fact that he confused technicians with *auruspices* or "watchers of omens," he shows quite clearly how the navigation department of a large ship at that time was organised and run. Aboard a small Turkish galleot there would not have been such a complement of specialists—possibly two or three, including the rais, or master.

Felix Faber also mentions the charts used by the mariners as being marked "in a scale of inches showing length and breadth," and describes the rhumb lines which were delineated on most charts of that period. Certainly there can be no doubt that the Turkish captains of Barbarossa's time did not wander vaguely over the sea, were far from incompetent in their navigation, and were perfectly able to rendezvous at a chosen place without much difficulty. All this adds up to a fair skill in navigation and a fair skill in their chart-makers. Quite apart from the fact that in the comparatively small area of the Mediterranean there was not much call for astronomical navigation—the ancients had got on well enough by simple observations of the Pole Star at night and the rising and the setting of the sun to give them a direction —the galley masters had so expert a knowledge of their vessels' capabilities that they could rely very well on dead reckoning. There are also no tides worth speaking of in the Mediterranean, which makes calculation by dead reckoning much simpler and more accurate than in the oceans.

They did, however, have a simple and ingenious instrument for measuring their latitude, the *kamal*. This was no more than a small wooden tablet, in its simplest form with a knotted string through the centre. It worked upon the principle that "an object of fixed length will measure the height of any heavenly body above the horizon according to the distance at which it is held from the eye . . . In the simplest instruments the user had the known star altitude for each port on his route knotted on the string and recognised them according to each length found. But more usually the string was knotted at distances corresponding to *isbas* of 1° 36′, each four of which make a *dubban* of 6° 24′ . . ." The *kamal* was a forerunner of the cross-staff, which was also in wide use by the sixteenth century.

It is evidence enough of Barbarossa's capabilities at sea that we never hear of any vessels being lost by stranding throughout his campaigns. Also, unlike the Spaniards, who were constantly falling foul of the treacherous coastline and weather of North

Africa, the ships under Barbarossa's command do not seem to have been hazarded on expeditions at unsuitable seasons of the year.

A great sea captain must also be a considerable navigator, and there is no doubt that Barbarossa, like Drake, had mastered the art of navigation long before he became the Commander-in-Chief of the Ottoman fleet. Although his service was in the hot, tideless Mediterranean, and not on the great oceans of the world, he, too, had learned from his youth onward, by the true symbiosis of sailor and sea, the feel of the winds and weather. He knew in the palms of his hands the dead swell from an old storm centre, the new swell presaging wind on the way, the movement of coastal currents, and the pattern of solar winds. He knew the *marobbio* that, suddenly and without any warning, can surge round the southern coast of Sicily, raising the sea level two or three feet in calm weather. He knew the khamsin or gibleh when it blew hot as a furnace off the deserts of North Africa and then, picking up moisture as it moved over the sea, turned into the sirocco that plagues the Maltese archipelago as well as all southern Italy and Sicily.

The Sultan's new Admiral was, like all great sailors, familiar with all the aspects of the sea—so much so, that he seemed as much a part of it and it of him as if their natures were indissolubly linked together. He knew in himself the violence and the fury, and the long calms of easy weather. He knew, too, its indestructible energy. It is hardly surprising to read that, all that winter, "Barbarossa was continually in the arsenal, where he did both eat and drink to lose no time."

13

TRIUMPHANT SUMMER

In July 1534 the Turkish fleet left the Golden Horn with its new Admiral in the van. It moved by easy stages down through the Aegean, to turn west round Cape Matapan. The inhabitants of the islands saw them pass. They clustered together in their hilltop villages (for the ancient harbour towns along the coasts had long since been abandoned) wondering, no doubt, whether the Turks were in search of more Christian sons to make into janissaries, or whether some expedition was planned to carry off their young men for service in the galleys. From the white Chora of Samothrace to the Chora of lonely Amorgos they watched the procession of this great new fleet as it made its way southward through the sea that their forefathers had once called "the Sea of the Kingdom." But the kingdom to which it now belonged was that of the Ottoman Turks, whose empire now extended to Tabriz in Persia. The one-time invaders of Europe, whom the ancient Greeks had defeated in the most glorious years of their history, were now powerless; even the Persians were in retreat before the Turks. As John Milton phrased it:

Bactrian Sophi, from the horns
Of Turkish crescent, leaves all waste beyond
The realm of Aladule, in his retreat . . .

Now the crescent horns of an advancing line of galleys and galleots moved westward through the Ionian Sea, bound for the trouble of Europe and equally for the discomfiture of the Moslem ruler of Tunis. Eighty-four ships, according to one account, left Constantinople that summer under the command of Kheir-ed-Din Barbarossa.

The ports and coastal villages of Italy and Sicily had learned in the past to look southward for the lean hulls of the galleys from the Barbary Coast, for the lateen sails and the fourteen-a-side oars walking deliberately and purposefully towards their shores in the summer months of the raiders. Their watchtowers were manned along their coastlines and on their rocky peaks to give advance warning of the approaching enemy. From Malta and Gozo, from Sicily, from the Aegadian and the Lipari Islands, the local militia looked southward in the summer. But now, for the first time, to their horror the enemy struck suddenly from the east—and not just a few marauding corsair captains, but a huge fleet organised and commanded by none other than Barbarossa.

Setting his course westward from the coast of Greece, Barbarossa arrived out of the blue Ionian like an earthquake on the earthquake-ridden Strait of Messina. Here, in the region once haunted by Scylla and Charybdis and described by Homer as the place where "no sailors can boast that they ever passed Scylla without losing some of their number," a new, but human, terror struck. Early one morning, out of the dormant sea, came the threshing sound of the galleys—poised on whose *rambadès* were janissaries with their bows, arquebuses, and scimitars. Swinging to the north up the Messina Strait, leaving Cape Spartivento behind them, they saw on their port hand the long range of mountains that back Messina, and far away on their quarter the lazily smoking peak of Mount Aetna. They were in the land of legend, but they brought their own legend with them—one that was to dominate the Mediterranean, in a sense, far longer than the poetry of Homer. They brought the legend of "the corsairs" and of "the Barbary Coast." This raid on Reggio was only a forerunner of the many that were to change the whole face of the Mediterranean coastline during the sixteenth century.

Reggio, a city that had remained faithful to Rome throughout the Punic Wars and which even the great Hannibal had never succeeded in taking, now fell into the hands of the Turks. For the first time the unfortunate southern Italians realised that the threat to their shores came not only from North Africa, but also from the Turks in the East. Barbarossa and his troops fell upon the city commanding the trade route between Italy and Sicily, and devastated it. Its inhabitants were enslaved—the young men destined for the galleys and the young women for the harems of Constantinople.

Moving northwards by easy stages up the Tyrrhenian Sea, they terrorised the Italian seaboard, even sweeping into small ports like Cetraro, to capture the local shipping and carry off the inhabitants. Communications were bad in southern Italy, and the news of Kheir-ed-Din's onslaught did not reach Naples in time. If it had, one must surely have expected the Viceroy to prepare his galleys for action, and to lie in wait for the Turks as they resolutely pressed on northwards. Surely from the watch posts on Anacapri, from the heights of Sorrento, and from ancient Amalfi (once itself ruler of these seas), the advance of so large a fleet must have been seen? But it may be that Barbarossa timed his passage to the west of the Bay of Naples for the dark hours. Certainly there was no naval engagement. Perhaps the Viceroy and his advisers knew that with their limited fleet there was nothing they could do to stop the raider's passage. Barbarossa, in any case, had vanished into the smoky blue seas to the north of the city. A few days later the news of his next exploit was brought to Naples by a sweat-stained horseman from the Gulf of Gaeta. Barbarossa had sacked the ancient seaport of Sperlonga—where the Emperor Tiberius had once had a summer villa—and had "loaded his ships with wives and maidens."

But Kheir-ed-Din had in mind a particular prize for the Sultan: something that would shine like a pearl among the simple treasures of his other captives. Twelve miles northwest of Sperlonga lay the ancient town of Fondi, the family home of the Counts of Fondi. The present Countess was none other than the renowned Giulia Gonzaga—descendant of one of Italy's greatest families, related to the late Pope Martin V, and the young widow of the noble Vespasio Colonna. Giulia Gonzaga's beauty had been celebrated by painters and poets to such an extent that rumour of it had even reached the Sublime Porte. The unfading amaranth, the flower of love, was the appropriate device on her coat of arms. What more suitable gift, then, could Barbarossa bring the Sultan than the lady herself—beautiful, nobly born, and highly suitable therefore for the Sultan's harem?

After leaving his troops to sack Sperlonga, Kheir-ed-Din with a raiding force moved swiftly up the road to Fondi. Fortunately for the lady, some advance news of the approach of the Turks must have reached her. Although she was in bed when a messenger stumbled up to the villa, she just had time to leave the house, leap on her horse in her night clothes, and make her escape. In the words of Von Hammer in his *History of the Ottoman Empire:* "The attendant who accompanied her on this desperate midnight flight she later had condemned to death—saying that he had taken advantage of her distress and had been overbold." An illustration to the *Histoire des Pirates et Corsaires* shows Giulia Gonzaga, with a sword in her hand and her breasts bare, riding down a Turkish soldier while the town of Fondi goes up in flames behind her.

Foiled of his prey, Kheir-ed-Din abandoned the town to his

troops. Hamilton Currey, with more imagination than documentary evidence, writes: "They sacked Fondi and burned the town; they killed every man on whom they could lay their hands, and carried off the women and girls to the fleet. Kheir-ed-Din was furious with anger and disappointment. 'What is the value of all this trash?' he demanded with a thundering oath, of the commander of the unsuccessful raiders, surveying as he spoke the miserable, shivering women and girls. 'I sent you out to bring back a pearl without price, and you return with these cattle.' "

The whole of his campaign that early summer on the west coast of Italy was designed, no doubt, to ingratiate himself with the Sultan. But it was also designed to lull the Sultan of Tunis, Muley Hassan, into a false sense of security. The news of the activity of the Turkish fleet on the coast of Italy was naturally spread far and wide throughout the Mediterranean. If Hassan had been suspicious that his neighbour, the Beylerbey of Algiers, was interested in his kingdom, he must surely have felt that he had nothing to fear from a man who was occupied with harrowing the Kingdom of Naples.

No doubt Barbarossa needed to use the Sultan's fleet to show some immediate return to the Treasury in Constantinople. The slaves and captured valuables went back in comfortable procession round Cape Malea, up the Aegean, through the Sea of Marmora, and into the quiet waters of the Golden Horn. Having shown this comparatively simple proof of his efficiency, Barbarossa was now free to add yet another dominion to the Sultan's glory—and to make himself its master. The fleet turned southwestward and headed for North Africa. They left behind them the green enamelled shoulders of the Italian mountains and passed Mount Erice towering above the western Sicilian coast. The lonely Aegadian Islands faded as they set course for the horned Gulf of Tunis.

On August 16, the fleet came to anchor off the Goletta, the "throat" of the great harbour of Tunis, and opened up a bom-

bardment of the entrance. There was no resistance. Muley Hassan, who had alienated his people by the fatal mixture of cruelty
and weakness, immediately fled. As Morgan puts it, "he packed
up as much of his treasure as he could and, with his women and
children, got away to his Arab allies in the country." Two days
later he made an ineffectual attempt at return, backed by one
thousand local horsemen, but the fire power of the Turkish
arquebusiers was too much for them. They scattered in panic,
and Muley Hassan escaped with them, to seek refuge in the
inland city of Qairwan. Tunis was Barbarossa's.

Thus, thirty years after he and his brother, unknown corsairs,
had been permitted by the then Sultan to shelter their two galleys in the Goletta, he returned to become King of the city.
Commander-in-Chief of the Ottoman Navy, recognised by the
Sultan Suleiman as the greatest Turkish sea captain afloat, ruler
of Algiers and of nearly all Algeria, Kheir-ed-Din was one of the
greatest monarchs in the Mediterranean world. As Sandoval
wrote in his *History of Charles V:* "From the Strait of Messina
to that of Gibraltar no one in any part of Europe could eat in
peace or go to sleep with any feeling of security."

The Sultan's galleys were now despatched to Constantinople,
laden with loot from their expedition against Italy. The greater
part of the janissaries were also sent back, having been well paid
by Barbarossa for their services. He kept with him his own galleys and some eight thousand Turks, renegades, and Moors. The
Christian slaves who formed his share of the captives were set to
work improving the defences of the Goletta, where a new fortress was built and a garrison of five hundred men installed.
Throughout the winter of 1534 the work went ahead. It was
rumoured that Muley Hassan was engaged in treating with
Charles V, offering to become his vassal if the Emperor would
recapture Tunis. Meanwhile, late into the year, the galleys and
galleots "were perpetually scouring the seas and coasts of Italy
. . . being in effect absolute masters in those quarters."

It was a bad winter for Europe. On all sides the power of the Ottoman Turks was threatening divided Christendom. Trade by sea had become so insecure that insurance rates in the Mediterranean were crippling. Venice imposed additional taxation to build new galleys to try to defend what was left of the city's trade with the East. But now that both Egypt and Syria were part of the Ottoman Empire, the great crescent of Turkish power had reduced the once-proud republic to a shadow of its former self. Genoa, whose western and central Mediterranean trade routes were now threatened by the Algerian Turks, was also compelled to raise taxes to construct fresh fortifications along the coast, and to build and arm new galleys. Many of the innumerable watchtowers and small forts that dot the coastlines of the Mediterranean countries and of the islands date from this period. Meanwhile, coastal towns and fishing ports began to fall into decay as more and more of the inhabitants removed themselves to the hilltop villages. Offshore fishing, once one of the main activities of islands like Sicily, Sardinia, and Corsica, was heavily affected—for only great courage, or hunger, could drive men down to their open boats to run the risk of being killed, sold as slaves, or ending up on a Turkish oar bench.

The reign of the corsairs had begun, and although the events of the following year might seem to alleviate Europe's distress, the pattern of life in the Mediterranean had now been so altered by Barbarossa that it would be centuries before normal conditions of trade would return. This sea, which had not been united since the days of the Roman Empire, and which had subsequently been disputed over by as many as twenty different states, was now—except for Spain and its possessions—predominantly Turkish. This astounding change in the heart of the Western world had been almost entirely brought about by two men, Aruj and Khizr, or Kheir-ed-Din, Barbarossa.

14

TUNIS LOST–MINORCA
STORMED

It is possible that Barbarossa had overreached himself in his sei-
zure of Tunis. Alternatively, if he intended to make sure of his
new territory, he should have retained the Sultan's ships and
janissaries. But this may not have been possible, for Suleiman
was engaged in his war with Persia (one of the few strategic
mistakes in his reign), and could not afford to leave so many
valuable men in North Africa. Barbarossa, also, had most probably calculated that in view of the divided state of Europe, even
Charles V would find it difficult to mount a large-scale expedition against Tunis. In this he was to be proved wrong.

Charles V could not ignore the threat that Barbarossa's occupation of Tunis posed to his Sicilian possessions. If he allowed
the Turks to establish themselves in Tunisia he would soon find
that Sicily was untenable. It was less than one hundred miles
from the Cape Bon peninsula to the ports of Trapani and Mar-
sala, an easy striking distance for galleys. They could be across
the strait of Sicily in twenty-four hours, raid and devastate the
coastline, and be back in Tunis before the news had even
reached Palermo. Charles did not have so many war galleys at

his disposal that he could afford to keep a squadron of them permanently in western Sicily: something that would be absolutely essential if he were to leave Barbarossa secure in Tunis. There was only one solution: to regain Tunis immediately and restore a ruler who would be a friendly vassal of Spain.

Muley Hassan was prepared to accept the Emperor's conditions in return for his restoration, and Charles either did not know or care that the exiled ruler was the most hated man in Tunisia. In any case, he wasted no time in setting everything in motion for an attack on Tunis at the first opportunity in the following year. The Marquis de Mondejar, Captain-General of Grenada, was ordered to raise men and money and set up camps for the troops outside the Andalusian ports. Andrea Doria, the Pope, and the Viceroys of Naples and Sicily and Sardinia were immediately acquainted with the imperial plan, and their help solicited or ordered as the case might be. The Knights of St. John, who held Malta in fee from Charles V, were also asked to lend assistance—something that they would have been unlikely to refuse in any case. Warfare against the infidel was their trade. Troops in Italy were told to prepare themselves for embarkation in the spring; orders were sent to Germany for the imperial troops to hold themselves in readiness; other detachments from Naples and Sicily were trained for the assault on Tunis. The main body of the invasion fleet would come from Spanish ports in the west, while other ships would join up from Genoa, Palermo, Naples, and Cagliari in Sardinia. The operation was well planned. Remembering previous failures on the dangerous North African coast, Charles V and his advisers clearly intended to leave little to chance. It was possibly the fact that they now fully realised the extent of the Turkish threat to Spain (and did not dismiss it as no more than the activities of "a few pirates") which ensured the success of their expedition.

Kheir-ed-Din, for his part, was well aware that he had neither

enough men nor a sufficiently fortified city to be able to with-
stand a large-scale attack. In the early spring of 1535, he sent
fifteen of his large galleots down to Bône, a sheltered small harbour almost halfway between Tunis and Algiers. He had learned
from previous experience that it was fatal to allow one's ships to
be trapped in port by the arrival of a superior fleet. His whole
position upon the coast had been made possible by sea power,
and he had no intention of losing his prime weapon in the event
of Tunis falling. Clearly he must have been prepared to wait and
see whether Charles and his fleet could manage to make a successful rendezvous for their combined operation. He must also
have hoped that either inefficiency or some natural disaster
would break up the armada before it could get off the Goletta of
Tunis. But, if it were successful, he had now secured his fleet at
Bône and Algiers. He had an escape route ready if things went
wrong.

Late in May 1535, the Emperor and the main body of the
fleet set out from Barcelona. On June 10 they rendezvoused at
Cagliari with the Italian and Sicilian sections of the fleet and
army. The total number of ships that left Barcelona is said to
have been four hundred, while the fleet that finally set out for
Tunis is reported to have been six hundred. As De Grammont
recounts the events in his *Histoire d'Alger:* "They left on the
13th. of June, and arrived off Tunis on the 14th., and immediately attacked the Goletta; this had been well fortified, but the
city of Tunis itself was not. After a number of skirmishes Barbarossa came out into the open country with his Turks. At the
same time the local troops attacked the imperial army from the
rear and on its flanks. On July 14th., the Goletta was taken by
assault, and on the 20th., at the moment when battle was opened
between the forces in front of the city, 12,000 Christian captives
who were held in the town broke their chains, and, under the
command of a certain Captain Paul Simeon, attacked the janis-

saries, who were already tired and worn out by the struggle . . ."

The immediate success of the attack on Tunis was due largely
to the capture of the Goletta on the first day of the campaign.
The credit for this must go almost entirely to the redoubtable
Knights of St. John. The knights had come down from Malta for
the campaign with four of their fighting galleys, and with the
great carrack that was the flagship of their fleet. This was almost
certainly the largest fighting vessel in the world at that time.
Since it was her cannon that so swiftly blew to pieces the new
walls of the Goletta and made a breach for the knights' assault,
some description of this immense vessel seems appropriate.

It "had eight decks or floors, and such space for warehouses
and stores that it could keep at sea for six months without once
having occasion to touch land for any sort of provisions, not
even water; for it had a monstrous supply for all that time of
water, the freshest and most limpid; nor did the crew eat biscuit,
but excellent white bread, baked every day, the corn being
ground by a multitude of handmills, and an oven so capacious
that it baked two thousand large loaves at a time. The ship was
sheathed with six several sheathings of metal, two of which
underwater, were lead with bronze screws (which do not con-
sume the metal like iron screws), and with such consummate art
was it built, that it could never sink, no human power could
submerge it. Magnificent rooms, an armoury for five hundred
men; but of the quantity of cannon of every kind, no need to say
anything, save that fifty of them were of extraordinary dimen-
sions; but what crowned all was that the enormous vessel was of
incomparable swiftness and agility, and that its sails were aston-
ishingly manageable; that it required little toil to reef or veer,
and perform all nautical evolutions; not to speak of fighting
people, but the mere mariners amounted to three hundred; as
likewise two galleys of fifteen benches each, one galley lying in

tow off the stern, and the other galley drawn aboard; not to mention various boats of divers sizes, also drawn aboard; and truly of such strength her sides, that though she had often been in action, and perforated by many cannon balls, not one of them ever went directly through her, or even passed her deadworks."

If this leviathan served to remind the Turks that they still had much to learn about shipbuilding from such master mariners as the knights, they knew already "The Religion's" fighting spirit. They can therefore have been little surprised to find that in the assault on the breach it was the Knights of St. John who claimed the van. A knight of the French Langue, the Chevalier Cossier, led the charge. Soon, the eight-pointed white cross on the standard of the order was floating above the breached battlements. Even the janissaries fled in disorder before these indomitable men.

If it was the escape and revolt of the Christian slaves in the city which finally delivered Tunis into the hands of Charles V, it was this first sudden and triumphant assault on the Goletta that put the prize within his grasp. Even Barbarossa recognised the qualities of these opponents. It is interesting to see that as late as the eighteenth century (when the Order of St. John was on the decline), Morgan could describe how greatly they were still respected by their Moslem enemies: "They are good corsairs; they are *men;* and as such behave . . . Were they not Cross-kissing Christians, and so much our enemies as they are, they would be very worthy of our esteem; nay, the best of us would take a pride in calling them our brothers, and even in fighting under their command."

But now, with the fortress at Goletta captured, and the city behind him in the hands of the former slaves, Barbarossa realised that there was nothing left but to put into action his plan of escape. Together with his principal lieutenant, Sinan "the Jew of Smyrna" and Aydin, he and the rest of the Turks withdrew to

Bône, where their ships awaited them. It was Charles's great failure (and one which he and all Europe would regret for a long time) that he did not annihilate the Turks in this hour of victory. Now was the moment when, leaving the city in the hands of a limited number of troops, he should have hastened after Kheir-ed-Din and defeated him on the battlefield. Charles had the troops to do it, he had—temporarily at least—the command of the sea. Furthermore, he was operating in a territory where many of the inhabitants were no more hostile to him and his Christians than they were to Barbarossa and his Turks. That he failed to do so was the penalty he had to pay for the way in which European armies at that period were allowed to pillage any city that they had taken by assault.

If a city formally surrendered before a breach had been made in its walls, then a meeting would be held between the leaders of the besieging army and the principal citizens. The terms of the surrender would be worked out, and the imposition of monetary and other tributes would be formally agreed. But in the case of a city that held out after its walls were breached, and which clearly had no intention of surrendering, the rules of war allowed the attacker to hand the city over to his troops for three days and nights. In drink and rape and loot the soldiers then took their wages for their part in the campaign. If such was the case in Europe, it was not to be expected that any mercy would be shown to the city of Tunis, the capital of a Moslem state. The fact that it was the Turks, and not the Tunisians, who had provoked this act of retribution made no difference.

"The streets became shambles, the houses dens of murder and shame: the very Catholic chroniclers admit the abominable outrages committed by the licentious and furious soldiery of the great Emperor. It is hard to remember that almost at the very time when German and Spanish and Italian men-at-arms were outraging and slaughtering helpless, innocent people in Tunis

. . . the Grand Vizir Ibrahim was entering Baghdad and Tabriz as a conqueror at the head of wild Asiatic troops, and not a
house nor a human being was molested." Discipline in the Turkish army was infinitely more strict than in any of the European
armies. In their long years of conquest throughout Asia Minor,
Greece, eastern Europe, and the Middle East, the Sultans, the
Vizirs, and the Pashas of the Ottomans had learned that a ruined
city is a poor inheritance. They preferred to pay their troops;
only permitting them to loot on special occasions, and then only
for a strictly limited period of time. The Turkish soldier feared
his officers and his sergeants more than he feared the enemy.
This efficient way of ensuring discipline was one that was to be
adopted by many Western armies in later centuries.

Tunis, recaptured for the benefit of Spain, was now handed
back to Muley Hassan. The fortress at Goletta, once it had been
made secure, was to become a Spanish possession, with a Spanish garrison (just as the Peñón at Algiers had formerly been).
An annual tribute was exacted from the restored ruler of the
city, no Christians were to be among the slaves, and no Turks or
other corsairs were to be permitted to use the harbour as a base
for their activities. It seemed, on the face of it, a great victory,
and the Emperor Charles V's conquest was well celebrated in
Europe. Barbarossa had been defeated. Thousands of Christians had been freed, and the threat to Mediterranean trade in
the narrow strait of Sicily seemed to have been eliminated. Unfortunately for Spain and Europe, the failure to follow up his
initial success rendered hollow the whole of Charles's campaign.

Morgan has it that Barbarossa was now urged by his followers to withdraw altogether from the western Mediterranean:
"Several of his captains proposed to him, that it was advisable
for them to make the best of their way to the Levant, in order to
solicit the Grand Signior's aid, to recover what they had lost;
since they could not think it in any wise safe for them to pretend

to abide in those Western Seas, where, sooner or later, the Emperor would not fail working their destruction. At this discourse, Kheir-ed-Din, being highly incensed, angrily replied: 'To the Levant did you say? Am I a man to show my back? Must I fly for refuge to Constantinople? Depend on it, I am far more inclined to go to Flanders.' And so, without communicating his intention to any, he commanded them all to follow his galleot . . ."

The dialogue, of course, is invented—or perhaps no more than oral tradition—but in any case it has the right ring about it. Certainly, we know the details of Barbarossa's next action. Far from taking any notice of the fainthearts among his lieutenants and supporters, he at once opened an aggressive war against the Kingdom of the Emperor. As on other occasions in his life, Barbarossa showed all the qualities of a master strategist and tactician. If he was often prepared of his own volition "to withdraw in order to jump farther," he was also aware that on the occasions when an opponent has forced one to withdraw, he little expects that one will use this withdrawal period in order to begin a new act of aggression. Barbarossa, having ordered his galley captains to follow him "without troubling to ask themselves questions," immediately put out to sea. It might have been expected that he would head for Algiers to reinforce the city, just in case Charles V decided to swoop back along the coast and complete his destruction of "the Turkish pirate." Far from it—the Admiral's galley set out on a northwest course into the Mediterranean.

No one in Spain or in its island off-riders, the Balearics, had any thought or concern for the Algerian corsairs. They knew well enough that Charles V was down off Tunis with a huge fleet, bent on destroying Barbarossa and removing all threat from their shores and sea lanes for ever. They had nothing else to fear in the native seas of the Catholic Emperor so, no doubt, their watchtowers and their guard posts were practically unmanned when the strike force arrived. Beating swiftly along the lazy summer sea came Barbarossa's fifteen galleots from Bône, together with a number of others that he had summoned to join him from Algiers. The elated inhabitants of the Balearics, gazing southward from the crags of Formentera, Ibiza, and Mallorca, were in no doubt that this was part of the imperial fleet, detached from the main body to water and revictual. "All this was no more than what the insidious Kheir-ed-Din had projected; for the better to beguile and confirm them in their error, he hoisted Spanish and Italian colours . . ." Passing the southern Balearics, the squadron made its way to the north, rounded Minorca and swept into the great harbour of Mahon on the north coast of the island.

"In fine settled weather," says the *Admiralty Pilot,* "anchorage can be obtained off the entrance to the harbour." But these incoming vessels had no intention of anchoring. A large Portuguese merchantman was lying there placid as a goose, and fired a friendly salute to the "Emperor's ships." This was returned by a thunder of shot from the bow chasers, a crackle of arquebus fire, and a hail of arrows. Despite a brave resistance by the astounded Portuguese, the ship was taken. The Turkish squadron now bore up towards the sleepy town of Mahon, tucked in its comfortably defensive elbow of water. They swept past the islets that glow green in that pleasant bay, ignoring such unimportant plunder. Off the shelving shore near the town they turned at the command of whistles, gongs, and the crack of lashes, to come in stern first towards the shore. Down went the gangplanks and out stormed the soldiers—an infuriated hornet's nest of men who had been driven from their pleasant home in Tunis to seek revenge.

While Andrea Doria, at the Emperor's command, was searching for Barbarossa along the North African coast, the latter was busy in the Emperor's domain. Port Mahon was sacked, six thousand were carried into slavery, and the defenses of the port and the great harbour were totally destroyed. Many cannon were carried off (some recompense for those that had been lost in the Goletta), and all the stores and valuables from the harbour warehouses were loaded aboard the galleots and the captured Portuguese merchantman.

Barbarossa had indeed lost Tunis, but he showed by this master stroke that he understood better than any in his day and age the proper uses of sea power. As they left the sacked city, the flames crackling against the night sky and lighting up the waters of its gracious bay, he is said to have turned to his lieutenants who had counselled him to be cautious and asked: "What think you then? Is this not better than going to the Levant?"

15

VENICE LEARNS A LESSON

Barbarossa had established the Kingdom of Algiers, and he left it a secure dependency of the Ottoman Empire. He had failed to hold Tunis, but its loss was to become relatively unimportant within his own lifetime. Muley Hassan did not live long to enjoy his vassalship to the Emperor, and his successors soon saw that their fortunes were linked with those of Turkey and not those of Spain. Kheir-ed-Din Barbarossa, whose initial fortunes had been founded upon the sea, was now to retire from the land and devote himself almost entirely to his native element.

Leaving the administration of Algeria in the hands of his friend and confidant the eunuch Hassan Aga, he set sail for Constantinople in the late autumn of 1535. For over thirty years he had lived in North Africa, and had made the western Mediterranean his home. Now he left the area where he had made Barbarossa a name with which Christians frightened their unruly children. He went back to the waters of the Levant where he had spent his early youth. He never saw Algiers again.

Morgan says that the reason for his withdrawal was that "regretting the loss of so fine a state as that of Tunis [he was]

147

determined personally to solicit Sultan Suleiman for a powerful reinforcement, in order to its recovery." There are no known records, and although it is possible that Barbarossa hoped to get the Sultan to lend him a number of ships and a force of janissaries to regain Tunis, the Sultan had more important projects at hand for his greatest sea captain. In that first winter in the dockyards of Constantinople Barbarossa had shown that he not only knew about ships, but that he had outstanding administrative ability. The Sultan needed a High Admiral, and he needed a thoroughly efficient navy. In recent years, the Venetians and the Genoese had been increasingly active in the Ionian and the Adriatic. The capture of Patras, the occupation of Modon, the imposition of a Spanish garrison in the fort commanding the narrow entrance to the Gulf of Corinth, all these showed Suleiman that, strong though he might be on land, he needed a powerful navy to secure his coastlines. Barbarossa, Beylerbey of Algiers, was now officially summoned home to take command of the Ottoman navy. He had established a Turkish dependency on the flank of the principal Christian power, the Kingdom of Spain. He was now to be asked to hang a Turkish fleet like a leech on the long leg of Italy.

In the spring of 1536 an event occurred which, although it had little effect on Barbarossa's career, cannot be omitted since it was symptomatic of an illness that would ultimately serve to destroy the Ottoman Empire. Ibrahim, the Grand Vizir of Suleiman, was murdered at the instigation of the famous (or infamous) Roxelana. The daughter of a Russian priest and a Russian mother, Roxelana had already persuaded Suleiman to have his son Mustafa murdered, so that her own son Selim (ultimately Selim II, known as "Selim the Sot") might inherit the throne. The murder of Ibrahim was promoted by Roxelana's desire that his place as Grand Vizir should be taken by her son-in-law, Rustem Pasha. Ibrahim had been a model Grand Vizir and was a man of exceptional intelligence and ability. His death was Turkey's loss and her enemies' gain. With Roxelana, the harem Sultana, there began that disastrous influence of women on Turkish affairs of state which was ultimately to weaken the whole administration of the Empire. The boudoir politics of eighteenth-century France were almost petty, and certainly comparatively civilised, compared with the intrigues in the seraglio. There, like a nest of female spiders (each intent that only her own offspring should survive and inherit), the favourites of the Sultans were to weave their webs of murderous intrigue.

It was on Ibrahim's advice that Kheir-ed-Din had been appointed High Admiral, and everyone who had been favoured by the late Vizir now came under suspicion. But political power and influence within the Ottoman court were of little interest to Barbarossa. He had learned over the past thirty years how to survive against Spaniards, Italians, Algerians, Moors, and Berbers alike, and he had no intention of running his head into a noose, however silken it might appear. Fortunately for him, Roxelana had no ambitions for any of her relatives in the fleet. Even more important was the fact that, although he owed his position to Ibrahim, Barbarossa's own policy for the use of the navy he was building was in complete opposition to that of the late Vizir.

Ibrahim had been born a Venetian subject in Dalmatia, and had always maintained an affection for Venice, with the result that during his years of office friendly relations had been maintained between the two powers. This was the reason why many of the Aegean Islands, Crete among them, had remained Venetian possessions and had been untroubled by the Turks. Barbarossa, on the other hand, having established Turkish sea power in the western and central Mediterranean, was resolved to eradicate the Christian powers from the Levant, the Aegean, and the

Adriatic. It must have seemed irrational to him that it was only in the waters nearest Turkey-in-Europe that the Ottoman flag did not reign supreme. Seeing that Suleiman's policy was to extend his empire steadily westward into Europe, Barbarossa had no difficulty in pointing out to the Sultan that, to realise his ambitions, he must have the sea lanes nearest his possessions under complete Turkish control.

Previously it had been the Spaniards and the Genoese who had been Barbarossa's main enemies, but now their place was taken by the Venetians. Although the Republic of Venice and the Sublime Porte were technically at peace, some foolhardy Venetians had recently taken to raiding the Sultan's ships on passage between Constantinople and North Africa. If the Sultan was affronted by this, his new Admiral was furious. He could not allow these "Cross-kissing Christians" to behave in his master's waters as he himself had been doing for so many years out of Algiers and the Barbary Coast. Throughout 1536 the shipyards and the arsenals of Constantinople were a hive of activity.

As if to provoke the Sultan and his High Admiral even further, Andrea Doria now had the temerity to sally out of Messina with a force of twenty-five galleys and capture ten Turkish merchantmen. Not content with this, having secured his slaves and his looted cargo back in Sicily, he made his way across the summer Ionian Sea. Doria was at this time seventy years old and an impressive figure of a man (even if politically he was as guileful as Machiavelli's ideal Prince). He had been largely responsible for Barbarossa's expulsion from Tunis, and he was now bent on carrying the war into the enemy's territory.

Ten miles south of Corfu lies the small island of Paxos. It was in these waters that, many centuries before, a naval engagement between the ancient Corfiote Greeks and the Corinthians had precipitated the fatal Peloponnesian War that was to be the ruin of Athens (now no more than a poor Turkish village). Into this same area there swept the galleys of Andrea Doria, to inflict a sharp defeat upon a section of the Turkish fleet under the command of the Lieutenant to the Governor of the Dardanelles. At the conclusion of the action, the captured Turkish galleys were towed through the narrow entrance channel into the little harbour of Paxos. The native Greeks and the Venetians who manned the harbour defences of the island were overjoyed to see the hated Turks ironed and set to work at the oar benches of the victor.

It is certainly true that until the advent of Barbarossa upon the Turkish naval scene the conduct of the Ottoman ships and their commanders seems to have been inefficient in the extreme. This was all to change, and in the very near future. But for the moment the indignity of this defeat was deeply felt in Constantinople. The Sultan, and his High Admiral in particular, felt that something must be done to wipe out the loss and the disgrace which Doria's two new successes had inflicted. Barbarossa had been given the men and the materials; he had brought with him his reputation for being the foremost seaman of his time; it was up to him to justify his name and his position.

In May 1537 Kheir-ed-Din Barbarossa led the Turkish fleet out of the still waters of the Golden Horn. With over one hundred galleys behind him (some accounts say as many as two hundred) he now had the means with which to achieve his ambitions. The Turkish plan was well thought out: a sea attack on the east coast of Italy and a sweep up the Adriatic, while the Sultan himself took an army of twenty thousand men across to Valona in what is now Albania. The plan was for the Sultan and the army to be transported across the narrow strait between Valona and Brindisi and, having captured that great and ancient seaport, to sweep northwards through Italy. The Governor of Brindisi, who was on the Sultan's payroll, was prepared to open the gates of the city to the Turks. In the event, the plan miscarried, because the Governor's treachery was discovered a few days before the attack was due to be launched.

But Barbarossa, meanwhile, in the words of one chronicler, "laid waste the coasts of Apulia like a pestilence." Andrea Doria, who was at Messina with his galleys, does not seem to have dared to intervene. His fleet was not strong enough to take on the force that Barbarossa had built up over the past twelve months. With thousands of slaves aboard and his holds filled with plunder, the High Admiral reluctantly obeyed a recall from the Sultan. The latter had decided, in view of the rupture of relations with Venice, to lay siege to Corfu, most important of the Ionian Islands and a Venetian possession since the division of the Byzantine Empire in 1204.

Despite the fact that the Sultan landed his whole army and thirty cannon—including a monster fifty-pounder, then the largest piece of ordnance in the world—the castle and fortifications of Corfu were still resisting when the approach of autumn determined the withdrawal of the troops and the ships. At first glance, the year's campaigning had not been very successful. Neither Brindisi nor Corfu had fallen to Turkish arms. But Barbarossa's earlier raid into Apulia, which had yielded so many slaves and so much plunder, was now to be overshadowed by his devastating sweep down the Ionian and into the Aegean.

Paxos, so recently the scene of Andrea Doria's triumph, was captured and most of its inhabitants were enslaved. The other Venetian possessions in the Ionian were similarly harried by these raiders from the sea, who proved even more terrible than the earthquakes that regularly plague life on those rocky, olive-starred islands. Rounding Cape Matapan, as the fleet made for its winter headquarters in the Golden Horn, Barbarossa raged through the Aegean more terribly than even the storms of winter. Almost every island that belonged to the Venetians suddenly found that its long years of peace with the Ottomans were at an end. Their trading vessels were seized, their young men put to the oar, and their young women abducted for sale in Constantinople. As if all this was not enough, they were now told that they must pay a yearly tribute to the Sublime Porte if they did not want a further visitation.

Venice had been in conflict with the Turks before, but this was the first time that she had ever had to deal with an Ottoman fleet that was well built, well manned, and led by Barbarossa. How bitterly the Republic must have rued the day when they had been so foolish as to invite this conflict. Venice subsisted by seaborne trade and anything that interrupted this was disastrous for her. Although for nearly two centuries more she was to maintain possessions in Greece and the islands (losing here, recapturing there, and always putting up a brave fight), yet the writing was on the wall for Venice from the moment that Sultan Suleiman called Barbarossa home to reorganise and build up the Ottoman fleet.

The High Admiral entered the Horn to a triumph such as had never been witnessed in those waters in the history of the Porte. It was true that many a Sultan and his armies had returned victorious to the city, at the head of the defeated, having enlarged the Empire by yet another province. But these had all been military victories. It was something novel for the inhabitants of Constantinople to see that ships could secure equal prizes to armies. When Barbarossa returned, in the words of Hajji Khalifa, "to rub his countenance against the royal stirrup," he brought with him 400,000 pieces of gold, 1000 young women, and 1500 youths. As a personal present for his lord and master he despatched 200 boys dressed in scarlet carrying vessels of gold and silver, and a further 200, some carrying bales of cloth and others holding before them embroidered purses heavy with coin.

"The creator of the Turkish navy, its admiral and its soul," as Duro remarked of him in his history of the Spanish navy, had more than avenged his Sultan's withdrawal before the walls of Corfu. But his actions in this campaign must not be seen as little more than a large-scale piece of piracy. Venice had provoked the war with Turkey, and it was in his capacity as Commander-in-Chief of the Sultan's fleet that Kheir-ed-Din Barbarossa had taken the war into Venetian territory. His violence was part of his age and time, and, as has been seen at Tunis, was far from being confined to "the terrible Turks." Indeed, a French ambassador later commented on Barbarossa's fleet that there was a discipline and order to be observed in the Turkish galleys which their European enemies would be wise to copy.

The fact that France had concluded an alliance with the Ottomans need not make one suspect the ambassador of any particular bias. Even the Knights of Malta, those eternal enemies of all Moslems, accorded Barbarossa and his successors a respect that they never gave to pirates. In the Wars of Religion, the Grand Master of the Order of St. John was, except for the fact that he was a Christian, occupying a position almost identical to that of Barbarossa. Grand Master La Valette (who was so successfully to defend Malta against the Turks in 1565) had himself served a period at the oars of a Turkish galley. It was no more than what might be expected if you lost in a sea battle. It is reported of La Valette that, stepping aboard a Christian galley on one occasion, he found the great Dragut among the oarsmen. He remarked to him in kindly encouragement: "It is the custom of war, Señor Dragut," to which the Turkish corsair replied, "Yes, and change of fortune." It was a hard world. No man in it suffered from the illusion that he possessed any "rights"—except those which his own brains and strength might possibly secure him.

The Franco-Turkish alliance had been secretly concluded in 1536. France's part in this, as a Christian nation allying herself with the Moslem enemy, has often been denounced. Sir Godfrey Fisher in his *Barbary Legend* has succinctly stated the pros and cons of the French behavior: "Francis I, with his erratic conscience and unpredictable changes of foreign policy, hardly appeared to advantage as a Paladin or champion of Christendom . . . The special denunciation of Turkey, and eventually of Algiers, arose out of the existence of the Franco-Turkish alliance, usually assigned to the year 1536, which is represented as essentially wicked and 'unhallowed', the source, it is claimed with a singularly ungrateful lack of realism, of so many of the misfortunes of France. More logically, perhaps, any sense of shame might have been derived from the discreditable state of affairs created by the duplicity and insatiable ambition of the princes, popes, and republics who showed no hesitation in paying tribute to the Sultan for his favour and protection, or invoking his aid against each other. The mutual recrimination and public washing of dirty linen must have been largely responsible for the contempt in which, according to Haedo and later writers, the Turks held the Christians."

It was indeed hardly surprising that the Turks despised the Christians. Everywhere they saw them professing one thing and doing another. If the intrigue in the seraglio of Constantinople was contemptible, it was little worse than in the courts of Europe. If France, through fear and hatred of the Emperor Charles V, wanted to come to a private agreement with the Sublime Porte, the Sultan's ministers were perfectly willing to oblige. Barbarossa had spent many years in the western Mediterranean. He had met many men of all conditions from the European countries bordering on the Mediterranean, and he had no illusions about them. The Christians, despite all their protestations, were interested primarily in territorial and economic gain. Barbarossa's policy of siding with France in order to weaken the Emperor and ruin Genoa and Venice was thoroughly intelligent.

Throughout the winter of 1537, the arsenals and the dockyards were once again working at full pressure. The maintenance of the new fleet, its replacement and extension, were largely made possible by the financial success of the past year. The Sultan's expedition to Valona had been costly, but Barbarossa's ravaging of Apulia, and of the Ionian and the Aegean Islands, had yielded an over-all profit in men, matériel, and money. At the end of the year 1537 the Ottoman Empire was at the peak of its power. Europe—dissident, divided Europe—waited uneasily for the spring.

16

DEVASTATION OF THE
ISLANDS

The islands of the Aegean, barren and poverty-stricken as so
many of them are, shining like bare bones under the brilliant
sky, were once prosperous and fertile. Their spoliation had begun as early as classical times, for man had little or no understanding of the need to replace the trees he had cut down for his
ship- and house-building, in order to conserve the soil. Nevertheless, during the long centuries of Byzantine rule many of them
had regained a considerable prosperity; piracy was eliminated in
the Aegean Sea; agriculture was encouraged; and trade flour-
ished. Similarly, in many of the islands that had become fiefs of
rich Genoese and Venetian families after the partition of the
Byzantine Empire by the conquering Latins there was order and
prosperity. Islands like Chios, Samos, Mitylene, and many
others had benefited by the attentions of men who were interested in seeing that their possessions showed a profit. It is significant, for instance, that Hydra, now treeless and waterless,
was known in the sixteenth century as Tchamliza, "the Place of
Pines."

But under the rule of the Turks, who introduced the ubiquitous goat (that murderer of saplings), and who cared little so long as the islanders somehow or other produced their yearly tribute, the islands suffered that long decline which is only just beginning to be arrested in our own century. The war between Venice and the Turks now inflicted a new devastation upon many of the Aegean Islands that had, until then, survived in comparative peace and prosperity.

In the spring of 1538 Barbarossa again led out a fleet of over one hundred galleys, and descended upon the islands conquered the previous year, to demand the annual tribute. In passing, he did not neglect some of the smaller islands which were under Venetian or Genoese sway. The first to feel the power of the Ottoman fleet was little Skiathos, lying just off the southern tip of Euboea, and commanding the entrance to the Gulf of Volos. The long sand beach of Koukkonaries Bay invited the smaller vessels to beach themselves, while the larger galleys swept round the island to seize the main harbour on the south coast. Halfway between the harbour and Koukkonaries lay the castle and the small fortified township (known like all similar Greek walled places as *castra*). Attacking it on both sides, the Turks took no more than six days to batter its poor defences into submission, swarm in, and massacre the garrison. Then, leaving a number of janissaries in command, they took what men and plunder they could find in the island, and moved on to their next target.

Such was the pattern of this spring raid through the Aegean. The small fortified *castra* had no chance of holding out against the massive force of men and cannon that were deployed against them. One by one, the islands that had for so long contributed to the power and prosperity of Venice fell into Turkish hands. Skiathos had given the Turks the command of the important Gulf of Volos. The other islands of the Sporades group, Skopelos, Khelidromi, and Pelagos, would be easy to subjugate in due course. Moving forty miles south across the windy sea, the fleet next ravaged lonely Skyros, capturing the castle that belonged to the Venetian Dukes of Naxos. The lifeline of islands that Venice had established in the great days of her trade with Constantinople were one by one falling into the hands of the Sultan. It was the Republic's turn to learn the hard lesson that she had in her time taught many others: those who wish to trade far afield must either possess a powerful fleet or must be on good terms with the people in whose territory they are trading. Venice's fleet was nowadays no match for the Ottoman, and she had forfeited her friendly relationship with the Sultan.

South again from Skyros lies the long island of Andros, commanding the Doro Channel, which in its turn is the main shipping route from the north Aegean to Athens and the Cyclades. The island's importance had long been recognised by the Venetians and, under their protection, it was governed by the Zeno and Sommariva families. Although it was not until 1566 that Andros was to come totally under Turkish rule, yet it, too, was now forced to pay tribute to the Sultan, in lieu of a levy being made upon its man power. Other islands which were not as prosperous as Andros were forced to provide rowers for the oar benches.

Inevitably, since Kheir-ed-Din had set out to challenge the large galleys of the naval powers of Europe, he had been forced to abandon his early preference for small galleots manned solely by Turks. His raids in 1537 and 1538 on the Ionian and Aegean Islands were not dictated solely by a desire to extend the Sultan's dominions, but by the necessity of finding enough oarsmen for the huge fleet he was building. Although there are no certain records, it may be assumed that his own High Admiral's galley was manned by janissaries. At this time the whole janissary corps did not number more than twenty thousand men, so it is unlikely that men from this élite could be spared for many vessels other than the Admiral's flagship. At a later date, when the

159

corps of janissaries had been considerably expanded, it was quite customary for janissaries to be employed as oarsmen. In Barbarossa's fleet a leavening of janissaries among the slaves was found not only to improve their discipline and performance, but to provide an "ear" against the slave revolts that were always one of the terrible concerns of the officers and masters of a galley. If, in a sea fight, the slaves managed to break or slip their chains, then the ship would almost automatically be overwhelmed. To have some janissaries among the crew was, therefore, a good insurance policy.

Moving southward through the islands, Barbarossa and his ships passed the lofty sides of volcanic Santorin and came down through the Sea of Crete to complete their complement of oarsmen. Crete had been a Venetian possession since 1204, and its capital, Candia, was one of the principal ports in Venice's eastern communications chain. The Turks fell upon the city but, unable to reduce the fortifications, had to content themselves with capturing those inhabitants who had not had time to take refuge with the garrison. They then passed on down the coast, laying waste the small villages and fishing ports. Over eighty villages, according to one account, were put to fire and the sword, and their young men enslaved. The off-lying islands of Dia, Yianisadhes, Koufonisi, and Gaidhouronisi yielded their quota of sea-hardened fishermen for the benches. Gavdos, the ancient Clauda, saw the sails lift like great wings over the eastern horizon. It was here that St. Paul on his voyage to Rome had nearly come to grief prior to his ultimate shipwreck on Malta: "And when the south wind blew softly . . . they sailed close by Crete. But not long after there arose against it a tempestuous wind, called Euroclydon. And when the ship was caught, and could not bear up into the wind, we let her drive. And running under a certain island which is called Clauda, we had much work to come by the boat . . ."

It was while the Turkish fleet was casually sweeping along this southern coast of Crete, diverging occasionally to seize provisions from the fertile countryside, to water the ships, and loot what they could from the peasant villages, that a galleot came running down from the Ionian Islands with an urgent despatch for the High Admiral. The combined fleets of Venice, Genoa, and the Pope, under the over-all command of Andrea Doria, Admiral of the Emperor Charles V, were at sea. They had been sighted in the Adriatic, heading south towards the Ionian Islands.

This, or something like it, must have been what Barbarossa was expecting. He can never have believed that his actions of the previous year would be allowed to go unchallenged. Indeed, it would seem more likely that in his ravaging of Apulia and the Venetian islands in the Ionian and the Aegean he had been deliberately "trailing his coat." His immediate reaction to the news seems to confirm this. Far from withdrawing into the security of the Aegean, he gathered his fleet about him and headed northwest for the Ionian. He had recently been reinforced by a contingent of some twenty galleys from Egypt, among whose commanders were the formidable Sinan, Murad, and Salah, as well as Dragut. The arrival of the Egyptian squadron was certainly no accident. One can reasonably assume that all Barbarossa's actions had been deliberately designed to lure Doria and the fleets of Venice and the Emperor down into the Ionian—for a major "set-piece" sea battle.

On the west coast of Greece, north of the Gulf of Patras, and slightly north again of the island of Levkas lies the narrow entrance to the Gulf of Arta. Known in classical times as the Ambracian Gulf, this giant inlet of the Ionian Sea is about twenty-five miles from east to west, and ten miles from north to south. The entrance to the gulf is narrow and winding, little more than a quarter of a mile wide in places. Furthermore, it is barred by offshore sandbanks which are difficult for even small vessels to penetrate in fair weather, and almost impassable when the wind sets in from the north. Between these various hazards a channel, little more than a cable wide, permits the careful navigator to reach the safety of this inland sea.

It was off here, in 31 B.C., that the forces of Antony and Cleopatra were decisively defeated in one of the most important sea battles in history—the battle that gave the world to the future Augustus Caesar. By a strange coincidence, the Battle of Actium took place in the month of September, and it was once again in September that another great conflict to decide the fate of the Mediterranean was destined to take place off the Ambracian Gulf. This was the Battle of Preveza, called after the Turkish village that now dominated the narrow strait.

The assembly of the allied fleets of the Emperor was a long and slow business: something that was almost inevitable in the days when only oars and sails gave a man power upon the sea. The fleet that was sailing southward for Corfu—the news of which had brought Barbarossa up north into the Ionian—was only a part of the huge fleet that was intended to be used against him. Even so, it was an impressive collection of fighting vessels, with Vincenzo Capello leading the Venetian squadron and Marco Grimani the papal contingent, that was now gathering in Corfu roads.

Eighty-one Venetian vessels—galleys and sailing ships—were soon supplemented by the papal squadron of thirty-six galleys and an additional thirty galleys from Spain. This was a formidable enough array in itself. Numerically it should have been quite adequate to deal with Barbarossa's fleet, which consisted of about 150 ships altogether. But this time the Emperor wanted to be so superior that there could be absolutely no doubt of his chosen Admiral, Andrea Doria, utterly crushing the Ottomans. To ensure this superiority he had mustered together a further forty-nine galleys under Doria's immediate command. These should have already been down at Corfu, but they were held up waiting for what both Doria and the Emperor believed would prove their trump card. This was the arrival of no less than fifty large sailing ships or "galleons." These square-sailed fighting vessels, mounting a formidable number of guns, had already established their dominance over the Atlantic and the seas of the New World. It was confidently expected that their massive fire power could be used to destroy the Ottomans before their galleys ever had a chance to get to grips with the sailing ships.

"Nothing rots ships and men," Nelson would one day remark, "so quickly as lying in harbour." If this was true in the eighteenth century, it was even more true in the sixteenth, when standards of hygiene were notoriously low and when any great assembly of troops in camps and aboard ships almost inevitably led to disease. But quite apart from this danger, the uneasy relationships that existed between the various commanders were not improved by their delay in Corfu. Venice had few friends among the other Italian states, and her deadliest enemy for centuries had been Genoa. The Spaniards, for their part, had little love or respect for any Italians. Grimani and Capello, whatever their personal feelings towards each other, were now united in resentment against the absent Doria. It was bad enough, Capello must have felt, to be second-in-command to a Genoese—no matter how great Doria's reputation. But to be kept idling in Corfu while Doria, inexplicably as it seemed, failed to put in an appearance added insult to injury. While Barbarossa's fleet, with nothing but success in its wake, worked its way up the western coastline of the Peloponnese, the Italians and the Spaniards fumed and fretted in their anchorage.

If the object of the Emperor was to use his combined fleet to break the Turkish sea power once and for all, the Venetians— while naturally agreeing with this aim—were primarily concerned for the security of their Ionian Islands. Grimani's interest was for the papal dominions, and for eliminating the threat that the Turks posed to the western seaboard of Italy. The Spaniards, a long way from home, were the Emperor's men, but had no interest in pulling papal or Venetian chestnuts out of the fire. Curiously enough, it was Grimani rather than the Venetian Capello who first tired of the inactivity at Corfu and decided to make a raid southward into the Sultan's dominions in Greece. It is impossible to know whether this was purely an independent action, or whether it was concerted between Grimani and Capello in an effort to stir up the Turks and lure them northward. At any rate, Marco Grimani now led the papal squadron down from Corfu and struck at Preveza at the entrance to the Bay of Arta. This move was perhaps intended as no more than a lightning raid, although it is possible that Grimani wanted to find out whether the Turkish fleet was by any chance esconced in the great bay. In either case, he failed in his objective. The Turkish fleet was not in Arta, and he was forced to retire before the guns of Preveza fortress with some losses in men and damage to his ships.

The news soon reached Barbarossa, who was approaching from south of Zante and Cephallonia. He quickened his pace, hoping no doubt to catch the enemy somewhere in the open sea between Antipaxos Island and Preveza. But Grimani, after his brief incursion into the Sultan's dominions, had retired north to Corfu. Barbarossa turned his fleet to starboard and headed for the Preveza channel. Not since the forces of the future Augustus Caesar had entered these waters, over 1500 years before, had the inhabitants of the country around the Gulf seen so massive an assembly of ships. On they came, galley after galley, to the sigh, creak, and rattle of oars and chains; to the steady plash like summer rain as innumerable oar blades struck the water in unison; and to the rumble of tambours like distant thunder in the hills. Barbarossa was taking the Ottoman fleet up the winding channel and into the great Gulf of Arta, where he could withstand the assault of all the navies in the world.

He brought his fleet to anchor just inside the Gulf. The galleys were moored in a great semicircle with their bow chasers all pointed towards the narrow entrance between Port Vathi to the north and Actium point to the west. No hostile ship would ever be able to round that point and live—and, so narrow was the approach channel, only one ship at a time could navigate it. Barbarossa had chosen one of the strongest natural defensive positions to be found anywhere in the Mediterranean. As Hamilton Currey rightly pointed out: "Barbarossa now occupied the same position as did Octavius in his combat with Anthony. The role of the latter general was now taken by Doria . . ."

With the arrival of Doria and his squadron in Corfu, the scene was set for a conflict of giants.

17

BARBAROSSA CONFRONTS ANDREA DORIA

It was not until September 22 that the imperial fleet was at last augmented by the arrival of the fifty sailing ships which had been delayed by the long calms of midsummer. Now that the Mediterranean weather was beginning to break, and the winds to blow, the sailing ships were in their element. But the problem of a mixed fleet of this type was that the weather which suited the galleon did not suit the galley, and vice versa. Andrea Doria was in the position that was to vex many commanders until such a time as the predominance of the sailing vessel was definitely established.

On September 25, having waited for a favourable wind, he took a northerly under his stern and headed down towards Preveza and the Gulf of Arta. It was no accident that Kheir-ed-Din Barbarossa had already taken his fleet into the Gulf, and was waiting there for his enemy. Even so astute a naval historian as Lane-Poole in *The Barbary Corsairs* made the mistake of assuming that sea battles in the sixteenth century were fought by men who did not understand their trade:

"On September 25th. the allied fleets appeared off the en-

Preveza and the island of Levkas

trance to the gulf, and then for the first time Barbarossa realised his immense good fortune in being the first in the bay. Outnumbered as he was, a fight in the open sea might have ended in the total destruction of his navy; but secure in an ample harbour, on a friendly coast, behind a bar which the heavier vessels of the enemy could not cross, he could wait his opportunity and take the foe at a disadvantage . . ."

This is to suggest that a man who had made himself master of the western Mediterranean, who had created the Kingdom of Algiers and the Turkish navy, and who had proved himself over and over again a great sea captain, just "arrived" and took up his position in Preveza by sheer luck. It was not simply a matter of Barbarossa's "immense good fortune" that he was in the Gulf of Arta, behind the sheltering guns of Preveza fort, at the moment when Andrea Doria brought down the combined fleet past Antipaxos, through Gomaros Bay, to drop anchor off Preveza strait.

From a first glance at the chart, it might seem that Barbarossa was trapped in the Gulf of Arta, blockaded in the real sense of the word, but a man who has a friendly country behind him is in no danger of shortage of supplies. Quite apart from that, he was in an impregnable position. All he had to do was wait until the enemy made some false move, and then pursue his advantage. This, in fact, was exactly what he did.

The northerly wind which had sped the galleons southwards, and had pressed behind the lean sterns of the galleys, did not turn into the fearsome *bora,* that hundred-knot north wind of the Adriatic which might well have wrecked the whole fleet. Calm fell. The ships anchored comfortably under the sheltering arm of Preveza point. It is a distance of some three miles up the winding narrow entrance to Preveza and round the inlet of Port Vathi to where the Turkish fleet lay at anchor. Doria can never at any moment have considered taking his fleet up this hazardous channel, dominated as it was by the fort at Preveza—and then to emerge round Actium point straight into the full fire power of Barbarossa's galleys. In any case a great number of his vessels, particularly the large galleys and the deep-draughted sailing ships, could never have crossed the sandbars that cluster like knotted sinews off the approaches to the channel. Even as it was, the guide ship of the fleet, a large sailing galleon on the extreme left wing, was only anchored in two and a half fathoms. This meant that she had less than six foot beneath her keel. Also there was always a grave danger at this time of the year that a gale might blow up from the west, and catch the fleet on a lee shore. Doria's position was not a happy one.

Barbarossa, too, had his problems. There was the danger that Doria might disembark his troops and cannon and lay siege to Preveza. If he did so, there could be no doubt as to the outcome. The fort and the town walls were comparatively weak, and certainly not designed to withstand the weight of metal that Doria could bring to bear upon them. If Preveza fell then Barbarossa would indeed be trapped. From the heights commanding the channel, the imperial troops would be able to forbid him access to the sea, while at the same time they would be able to bombard his fleet. It was true that he could always withdraw deeper into the Ambracian Gulf, but that would be to little purpose if the shores were occupied by the enemy. Doria would then be able to bring nearly all his fleet (excluding some of the deepest-draught ships) up the Preveza channel in his own good time. If Doria was in danger of hazarding his fleet on a hostile shore, Barbarossa was in some danger of being trapped in the capacious, but narrow-mouthed, "lobster pot" of the Gulf.

Barbarossa also had political problems somewhat similar to those of Doria and his Venetian and Genoese commanders. Although he was High Admiral, he was still compelled to pay considerable attention to his senior commanders. Many of them considered that, as men who had always served in the established forces of the Ottoman Empire, they deserved to rank higher than this former corsair who had been appointed over their heads. Sinan Rais in particular, a fanatically brave but strategically ignorant warrior of the old Ottoman school, was among Barbarossa's principal critics. He and his faction maintained that they should immediately land as many men as possible and establish them in trenches on the shore opposite Doria's fleet. In this way, he argued, they would prevent the enemy from landing and attacking Preveza. Barbarossa was adamant that this would be folly, and that any force that came within range of Doria's cannon would be wiped out. If they were to lose a large proportion of their finest troops in this way, it would so weaken the fleet that any subsequent naval engagement might prove disastrous.

In the meantime, the course that Barbarossa feared was being actively discussed in a council of war held aboard Doria's flagship. Fernando de Gonzaga, General in charge of the imperial forces, was urging the Admiral to make a large-scale landing and capture Preveza. He pointed out that, since it was clear the fleet could not possibly advance up the channel commanded by the guns of Preveza, the logical action was to storm the fort, capture the heights, and spring the trap on the Turkish fleet. It was sound advice, but Doria rejected it. The grounds for his refusal to disembark the troops were similar to Barbarossa's. If they were to suffer heavy losses on the land, the fleet would be disastrously weakened for any sea fight that might then ensue. In view of the fact that he had an immense number of troops on board—many of whom were no more than passengers embarked for a military action—his argument sounds weak. But more cogent, and probably the real reason for his refusal to permit a landing, was his stated fear that if a gale blew up while the troops were ashore he would be forced to withdraw the fleet. The soldiers would be left unsupported in hostile territory, ultimately to be cut to pieces by Barbarossa's janissaries.

It was the weather—the danger of a gale—that really prompted the whole of Doria's conduct during this phase of the operations. He was rightly fearful of losing the whole fleet on the shores of Preveza and Demata Bay to the south, if either a westerly or a northerly gale should chance to blow. The whole of Doria's conduct during the series of operations that constitute the Preveza campaign must be seen in the light of the time of the year. It was late September, a period when the Mediterranean is notoriously unstable. This is the month when the calm conditions of summer break down in gales, violent electric storms, and dangerous local phenomena like waterspouts. By waiting so long for the sailing galleons, Doria had thrown away his chances of a successful campaign. He had arrived at the very time when most Mediterranean shipping tends to keep as near as possible to some secure harbour. August would have been the moment to bring Barbarossa to battle.

While Doria's advice seems to have been accepted without query by General de Gonzaga, Barbarossa, on the other hand, was less successful in restraining the fire-eating element among his military commanders. Much against his will, he was persuaded on the second day, September 26, to allow a force of janissaries under Murad Rais to land at Preveza. They made their way over the narrow neck of land down to the beach which lay opposite the combined fleet of Spaniards and Italians. It was just as Kheir-ed-Din had foreseen. No sooner had the troops begun to start entrenching themselves on the shore than the guns of the galleys and the galleons opened up. It was a massacre. The immense fire power of the galleons was something that few Turks had seen before. Barbarossa himself had never encountered it (although he was too well informed not to have heard rumours of its power and accuracy). It was probably the fact that men like Sinan and Murad were unaware that the Europeans could mount such heavy cannons in their ships which led to the debacle. Unable to entrench themselves, devastated by the hail of shot from the fleet, the janissaries under Murad Rais were forced to retreat in disorder. They left many dead behind them on the cannon-scarred sands.

Barbarossa's opinion had been amply, if sadly, justified by this unnecessary loss of men. From now on there was no more questioning his decisions. The military had learned the hard way. They had learned, too, that in any matters relating to warfare—whether on land or sea—the counsel of a man who had spent his whole life in battle, and who had achieved his current position through his ability, and nothing else, was not to be lightly disregarded.

On the afternoon of the same day Doria detached a squadron of his galleys and sent them south from the main body of the fleet across the mouth of the strait. Possibly it was an attempt to lure Barbarossa out from his safe anchorage. If so, the wily old seaman was not to be taken by so simple a ruse. Barbarossa, secure in his niche on the western shores of Greece, was like an octopus in a cleft of rock—ready to lash out with his tentacles if something really worthwhile was offered, but not to be tempted by a small and unimportant lure. He contented himself with sending down the strait an equivalent number of galleys to those that Doria was offering him.

A spirited but inconclusive action developed. Doria's galleys tried to entice the Turks out of the cover of Preveza point so that they could be destroyed by the heavy guns of the fleet, while Barbarossa's galleys tried to entice the Christians up the strait so that they would come under the guns of Preveza. Neither side was successful in its transparent manoeuvres. Apart from some exchange of shot at extreme ranges, no real action developed.

It was now clear to both admirals that neither had any intention of being provoked into a fight under disadvantageous circumstances. This meeting between the two greatest seamen of the period shows Barbarossa as an astute strategist and tactician. Conversely, Andrea Doria (whom the Italians have elevated into one of their principal naval heroes) is revealed as having made the greatest blunder of all—coming too late upon the field. Later events were to show him in an even less favourable light.

On the night of September 26–27, Doria decided to withdraw from his position outside Preveza. He was still rightly concerned at the possibility of being caught on a lee shore, and he had decided to head south: either for the shelter of Vasilico Bay in Levkas; or into the waters between Levkas, Meganisi Island, and the mainland of Greece. There can be no doubt that he expected to be followed. By leaving the Preveza area and swooping southwards (away from the Venetian islands to the north) he was posing a threat to the Sultan's dominions. Barbarossa could not for a moment afford to let this massive armada get down into the Gulf of Patras or—who could tell?—swing round into the Aegean and attack the Turkish mainland. Doria, indeed, had a large enough fleet even to attempt to invest Constantinople.

Though it is impossible to agree with his designation of Barbarossa as a "pirate," yet Hamilton Currey commented accurately on his actions during the inconclusive forty-eight hours at Preveza: "It may seem a contradiction in terms to speak of the moral courage of a pirate; but if ever that quality was displayed in its fullest degree it was exhibited by Barbarossa in the Preveza campaign. In his intellectual outlook on all that was passing, both inside and outside of the Gulf of Arta, in this September of 1538, we see Kheir-ed-Din at his best. Ever a fighter, he knew when to give battle and when to refrain, when to sweep headlong upon the foe, but also when to hold back and to baffle by waiting until the psychological moment should arrive. Around him Sinan Rais, Murad Rais, and half a hundred others of their kidney were clamouring; they hurled insults at his head, they heaped opprobrium on 'the corsair' . . . But 'the corsair' kept his head, and kept his temper."

Envious though many of the other commanders must have

been of Barbarossa's rise to fortune, it is doubtful, in view of his appointment as Commander-in-Chief by the Sultan, if they would have dared insult him to his face. But we know from other events in the history of the Ottoman Empire that the struggle for power among the upper echelons was pursued with violence and venom. It was the faction who believed in action at all costs that had forced Barbarossa to allow the useless landing of the janissaries.

On the morning of September 27 the Turks saw that the main body of the enemy had gone and that only a few stragglers were in sight, heading southward past Demata Bay down the long bare coast of Levkas. The order was immediately given for the fleet to up anchor and follow. There was a light northerly breeze blowing—ideal for Doria's sailing vessels—and Barbarossa could not afford to let a moment slip. The penalty for failure in those days was neither a peerage nor a seat on the board of some public company. The Sultan's executioner was always ready to divorce the head from the shoulders of those who failed to advance their master's cause.

18

TRIUMPH
IN THE IONIAN

Once again the narrow strait of Preveza was brilliant with the splendid procession of the Ottoman fleet. They came down in line ahead, galleys and galleots of the Sublime Porte, feathering the shallow water into foam as they rounded the point and headed for the open sea. Actium Point, which had witnessed the ruin of Antony's hopes and his ignominious flight with Cleopatra, was only destined to record the opening phases in the conflict between Doria and Barbarossa.

Doria and his ships were now strung out in a long line down the western shores of Levkas. While some were just clearing Demata Bay, others were rounding Cape Zuana, and others again were drawing near the islet of Sesola, some ten miles further south. If Doria's actions during the Preveza campaign must be criticised, it is only fair to point out that he was handling a combined fleet of galleys and sailing vessels—an almost impossible mixture, and one which was later to contribute to the disaster of the Spanish Armada against England. When the wind blew fair, the galleons would sway far ahead while the galleys dropped astern; but when the wind was foul, or if it was calm, the sailing vessels would hang idle and the galleys (in the very conditions for which they were built) were compelled to throw away their advantage and wait for the sailing vessels. This was exactly what happened now.

The fair northerly wind that had enabled Doria to withdraw his ships from Preveza began to falter and fail as the sun rose. Throughout the day, while the sailors worked their sails to catch every errant puff of air off the steep sides of Levkas, the galleys rowed and rested, rested and rowed, striving to maintain their squadron formations and not draw too far ahead of the galleons. Shrill twitterings filled the air (like birds restless at dawn) as the overseers' and under officers' silver whistles gave the orders for the manoeuvres.

These sounds were part and parcel of galley life. The slaves' first duty on joining the oar bench was to learn what every trill or series of pipings denoted. Jean Marteilhe de Bergerac wrote in his memoirs of his life as a French galley slave how "all the manoeuvres and all the tasks that one must undertake are indicated by different tones of the whistle . . . I remember how on one occasion our crew got hold of a lark and hung him up in a cage. The bird soon learned to copy the different whistles so well that quite often it would imitate them, thus causing us to undertake manoeuvres that had not been ordered. Finally the captain ordered us to get rid of the bird—which we were happy to do, for it wasn't giving us any rest . . ."

As it often will in that part of the world, a gentle breeze sprang up towards nightfall. As the land cooled, the sea wind began to draw back again over the stark inland mountains. The lighter sailing vessels of Doria's fleet were able to make their way a little further southwards. But, for the heavy galleons, this pale night wind was hardly enough to lift the sagging bellies of their salt-stained canvas. It was in this way, and for this reason, that the largest and most powerful ship in the fleet got left many miles behind the others.

A magnificent "battleship" of her period, known as the "Galleon of Venice," under the command of one of the most able Venetian seamen, Alessandro Condalmiero, could not find enough wind to maintain her way. Condalmiero was in over-all command of all the Venetian sailing ships, and his flagship was reckoned to be the most formidable warship in all the Mediterranean. Like the Great Carrack of Rhodes, the flagship of the Knights of St. John, the Galleon of Venice was built to a tremendous strength, sheathed with plate below, and carried an immense weight of cannon. But her deep draught, her over-all tonnage, and her somewhat cumbersome structure made her far slower than the other galleons, let alone the galleys. It was for this reason that Alessandro Condalmiero's flagship was last in the line of stragglers as Doria's fleet made its way slowly southwards towards Cape Dukato, the southern promontory of Levkas.

On the morning of September 28, the wind piped up foul from the south. Andrea Doria was in an uncomfortable situation. He brought his own flagship to anchor just off the islet of Sesola, but the position was useless as an anchorage for the fleet since deep water ran between Sesola and the nearby coast of Levkas. There were no harbours, no islets even, on all that steep coast. Some of the ships had anchored just offshore, others were five miles south of their Admiral off the precipitous white cliff known as Sappho's Leap (since the poetess was reputed to have jumped from it to her death). Others again were five miles or more north of Sesola, while the Galleon of Venice had still not rounded Cape Zuana, nearly ten miles away. So all the imperial fleet was now scattered in a straggling line up and down the iron-bound shores of Levkas. If Doria's action in leaving Preveza had been designed to draw Barbarossa out and engage him on the high seas, now was the moment to regroup his fleet, take the south wind under his stern, and head back north to meet the Turks. Yet, inexplicably, Doria did no such thing. He stayed at anchor off Sesola and seems to have made no attempt to regroup or to take any constructive action.

It was at this moment that the Ottoman fleet came into sight, rounding the northern tip of Levkas and hauling out of Demata Bay. Barbarossa's flagship was in the centre of a great line that curved slightly like a scimitar, Dragut holding the right wing and Salah Rais the left. Dead in their line of advance, formidable, dwarfing the lean galleys with its towering superstructure, lay Condalmiero's flagship. The light southerly that had checked the progress of the other sailing ships had not reached Cape Zuana. Up here the water was flat calm, not an errant cat's paw moving over its surface to disturb the ship's huge shadow.

Condalmiero, as soon as he saw the approach of the Ottoman fleet, sent back a rowing boat to Doria asking for his orders, and requesting that galleys be sent up to assist him in the action that must soon begin. As he was settling down to await the inevitable attack, the boat returned with the message that help would soon be on its way. Barbarossa's galleys hesitated before this immobile giant. They knew that they could never match her fire power with their light forward guns. The only solution was to attack in individual squadrons, coming in a wave at a time, retiring, reloading, and then returning.

The first squadron of galleys was immediately despatched against Condalmiero. He was a conspicuous figure on the poop of his ship, shining in full armour underneath the Lion Standard of Venice. In the first salvo one shot struck home against the mainmast, which crashed overboard in a tangle of rigging and canvas. Encouraged, the galleys came on as if to ram. They were encouraged, too, by the absence of any return fire from the great ship. Condalmiero had ordered his Venetian gunners to hold back until he gave the word. They were not to waste their fire, but to wait until there could be no doubt of their broadsides striking home.

So she lay there in the water, the great dark Galleon of Venice, with her gunners poised with their slow matches ready, and her upper-deck crew lying low beneath the bulwarks. Condalmiero had further ordered his gunners not to waste their shot by trying for individual targets, but to lay their guns in the line of the approaching vessels and use a ricochet effect against the galleys—rather like a boy skipping stones across the water. He had decided he was more likely to succeed by this method than by asking his gunners to try to drop individual cannon balls upon individual ships. His judgement proved sound. As the first wave of Barbarossa's galleys came within a few hundred yards of the motionless galleon, every gunport discharged a thunderstorm of flame and death. The new navy—the navy that was to triumph all over the world until the advent of steam, the navy of sail—showed in this first action of the Preveza campaign that it was the broadside with its solid weight of shot that now counted in warfare. Always, prior to this, it had been manoeuvrability and the ultimate act of boarding which gave one side or another the victory. This had been so since classical times. But the fact that sailing ships could now be built large enough to contain an armament about as heavy as that of a shore-based fortress was to change the whole aspect of naval warfare.

The first attack of the Turkish galleys was beaten off with heavy loss of life and considerable damage to the vessels. One of the galleys sank on the spot, several others were disabled, and all the calm blue sea became agitated with struggling men, ruined ships, toppling masts, and shattered discarded oars. The screaming slaves beat their chains against the benches as the shot tore in above their heads or smashed their oar blades to pieces. Wood splinters howled and sprang like vicious knives above and below the raked galleys. Like a pack of dogs, cuffed off and lacerated by a bear's paws, they withdrew beyond the range of the Galleon of Venice's guns.

Now Condalmiero began to play his guns with calm and deadly accuracy upon the circling galleys, not wasting shot, but waiting until a galley stopped, or began to turn—so that he and his gunners had a practically immobile target. Barbarossa, who was directing the action, immediately ordered his galleys to attack in squadrons from both port and starboard of the Venetian, but not to come within close range. He hoped that gradually the bow chasers would be able to riddle the great galleon and kill her crew, so that she would either sink or be compelled to surrender.

Meanwhile, where were Andrea Doria's galleys? He had been told before the action began that help would be required. It was ten miles from the main body of the fleet off Sesola Island to Cape Zuana, so at a striking rate of some four knots it should have been possible to get galleys to Condalmiero's assistance within two and a half hours at the least. Yet the long day wore on while the Turkish galleys sped in and out from the crippled giant, and no one came to her help. Even though the wind had dropped again and all his fleet of sail was becalmed (that sailing element upon which he and the Emperor had relied to give them an annihilating victory), yet Doria failed to provide the galley support he had promised.

In the afternoon, while the battle raged around the Venetian flagship, the wind settled down to a light breeze from the south. This should have been ideal for Doria to marshal his fleet and sail northward to destroy the Turks. He had overwhelming numbers, far heavier ships, and now he had a fair wind. Yet for over three hours the Genoese Admiral did no more than tack up and down off the coast of Levkas. As Admiral Jurien de la Gravière commented in his assessment of the action in *Doria et Barberousse*: "For far less than this the English shot Admiral Byng in 1756."

It is on record that both Doria's senior commanders, Marco

Grimani and Vincenzo Capello, went aboard the flagship and implored him to lead the fleet northward and engage the Turks with all his forces. After all, this was why they had combined. This was why they had waited so long at Corfu, so as to have the overwhelming fire power of the sailing galleons to destroy Barbarossa and the Ottoman fleet once and for all. But it was not until late in the afternoon of September 28 that Doria at last got the fleet under way and ordered it to sail northward. Even so, instead of going straight for the Turks, he hauled his line out to seaward as if daring them to follow him and meet him on the high seas, away from the dangerous coast.

Barbarossa had no more intention of accepting this lure than he had previously had of leaving Preveza. While the main body of his galleys continued their assault on Condalmiero's galleon, other galleys were thrashing down the coast to pick up whatever stragglers they could find. Barbarossa's conduct of his ships during this day again irresistibly reminds one of Drake's tactics during his harrying of the Spanish Armada up the Channel. With fewer ships than the enemy Barbarossa could not, and would not, let himself be drawn into a major fleet action. He contented himself with worrying the flanks of the enemy and picking off stragglers. His instinct and his conduct were right, and he showed himself in every way a superior seaman to Andrea Doria. No doubt, also, Barbarossa—who had a secure port at Preveza to which he could swiftly retire in the event of bad weather—hoped that a gale would spring up and destroy the Christians. In this respect he did not have Drake's luck. "The winds of God" failed to blow and scatter the enemy.

Doria's conduct during this day, on the other hand, seems inexcusable—so inexcusable that it has often been hinted that he wished as much as anything to see the Venetians weakened by the loss of their flagship. It is possible. One has to remember that the history of Doria's life reveals a man who was always capable of changing sides when it suited him, and who had a Machiavellian lack of scruple in politics. He suffered from the greatest defect that an admiral can have: he was a highly political animal, and he was a politician before he was a sailor. But, if one cannot bring oneself to believe that he deliberately left Condalmiero without assistance for political reasons, his behaviour seems incomprehensible. No doubt he would have preferred to fight a set-piece sea battle well out on the open sea, but can he have believed that Barbarossa would leave the coastal waters that suited his fast galleys, and allow himself to be engaged by a vastly superior enemy under the very conditions which suited the enemy's sailing vessels?

While Doria hauled out to seaward and, in Hamilton Currey's words, "executed useless parade movements," the Turkish galleys were busy snapping up any laggards that might come to hand before the sun set. In this way a Venetian galley was cut out from the end of a line, boarded, and captured. Meanwhile the unavailing onslaught against the Galleon of Venice continued, with squadron after squadron withdrawing to lick its wounds before the deadly fire of the huge warship.

By withholding his fire until the gunners were confident of their targets, and by using the ricochet effect with his cannon shot, Condalmiero achieved the most impressive success of the day. He demonstrated once and for all that a stout sailing ship, manned by well-disciplined seamen, was more than a match for any oared galleys. The successful defence of the Galleon of Venice in the Preveza action marked—for those who could read the signs—the writing on the wall for the Mediterranean galley. It seems that Barbarossa was intelligent enough to know when to cease wasting men and ships, for not long before sunset, when the Venetians were expecting a massed attack, the Turkish Admiral ordered his ships to withdraw.

Some historians have held this against Barbarossa as marking a failure of nerve. Certainly the victory was Condalmiero's, and the gallant Venetian managed to make his way northward overnight to the safety of Corfu. But senseless losses had never been to Kheir-ed-Din's taste, and in this he was in advance of most Turkish military thinking (Turkish leaders usually being inclined to use masses of men and material in simple "steamroller" techniques). He redeployed his galleys and, in the last hour before darkness fell, used them to cut out a number of smaller sailing galleons that had become detached from the main body of Doria's fleet. By the end of the day the Ottoman fleet had captured, as well as the Venetian galley, another galley, from the papal squadron, and five Spanish sailing ships. This was no small return for the sinking of one, possibly two, galleys, and for the disablement of several others. Not a single Turkish ship had been captured by Doria's forces and none had struck her colours. By his refusal to close with the far inferior Turkish forces, and to use his immensely superior fire power, Doria had thrown away all chances of victory. The field was Barbarossa's.

During the night the southerly breeze freshened. The Turkish fleet withdrew beyond Cape Zuana into the lee presented by the northern coast of Levkas. Doria, who had all the open sea northward to the Corfu channel ahead of his fleet, might well have heaved-to and waited for the dawn. Then, with the wind under his stern, he would have had the weather gauge of the Turks. But when the dawn came the Turks, to their astonishment, saw the whole of the imperial fleet heading northward for Corfu. Doria had withdrawn from the engagement.

His decision remains incomprehensible, and it is extremely difficult to see how, after the battle of Preveza, he ever managed to retain his commanding prestige with the Emperor. Sandoval, in his *History of Charles V*, says that Barbarossa, when retelling the story in later years, used to shake with laughter and maintain that Doria had even extinguished his admiral's lantern on the poop—so that no one could see him slipping away. The only excuse one can possibly find in mitigation of Doria's conduct is that he was a Mediterranean admiral, accustomed to galleys but with little experience in handling large numbers of sailing ships. The mixed composition of his fleet was a bugbear to him from the very start. It seems that his fear of losing the Emperor's galleons through bad weather on a lee shore crippled his courage and his judgement.

If the one occasion in their lives when the two most famous seamen of their time met with their combined fleets proved to be an inconspicuous engagement, there could be no doubt who had emerged the victor. In every respect Barbarossa had shown himself superior to Andrea Doria. He was outnumbered by nearly fifty ships, many of which had an individual fire power equivalent to a whole squadron of galleys. Yet he had seven captured vessels to his credit when Doria withdrew. He had shown his sagacity at Preveza when he had refused to be lured from his lair. He had outmanoeuvred Doria during the action on September 28, and but for the damage inflicted on his galleys by the inspired resistance of Condalmiero, he would have achieved all this with hardly any casualties.

While the imperial fleet was reanchoring in Corfu, prior to departing for the home ports of its various units (and it can be imagined with what feelings the Venetians left for the Adriatic) Barbarossa returned to Preveza. Relays of horsemen carried the news to the Sultan of the defeat of the Emperor's fleet, and of the flight of Andrea Doria and the combined forces of three great Christian powers. Suleiman the Magnificent was at Yambol in Bulgaria when the report of his High Admiral's victory finally reached him. He had the whole town illuminated as a mark of triumph and sent a despatch to Constantinople ordering processions to be made to Santa Sophia (once the heart of Eastern Christendom) and to the other mosques, to give thanks to

Allah for the success of the Sultan's arms. In recognition of the fact that it was above all Kheir-ed-Din's victory he increased his Admiral's annual income by one hundred thousand aspers.

By the time that the victorious fleet reached Constantinople there was no corner of the Ottoman Empire which had not heard how "the King of the Sea" had proved his right to that title. He had given the Sultan the mastery of the western Mediterranean, and he had now given him the mastery of the eastern basin as well. From the waters of the Black Sea to the Atlantic coast of Morocco there was no one to challenge the Sultan. His Admiral was supreme in the Mediterranean Sea, and had turned it for his master into "a Turkish lake." If the years from 1538 until the death of Sultan Suleiman in 1566 were the most glorious in the history of the Ottoman Empire, it was largely owing to Kheir-ed-Din Barbarossa.

19

GLUT IN THE SLAVE
MARKET

Barbarossa was blessed by fate in the last years of his life. For
him there was to be no decline in mental or physical vigour, nor
did he suffer any eclipse in fame and fortune such as bedevilled
the closing years of Francis Drake. Esteemed throughout his
own country as the greatest seaman in Turkish history, a fa-
vored confidant of the Sultan, and feared and respected throughout Europe second only to the Sultan himself, he was fortunate
enough to enjoy the success that he had earned. From Haedo
and from Morgan we learn that among other things, "he erected
and nobly endowed a most magnificent Mosque, and near it a
stately dome for his own sepulchre, about five miles from that
large suburb of Constantinople called Galata, not far from the
coast, a little before the mouth or entrance of Kara Dengis, or
the Black Sea: all which shore is adorned with most beautiful
and delicious gardens, vineyards and pleasure-houses, not unlike
the fine river of Genoa. At Constantinople, he likewise built a
very large and commodious Bagnio, or Public Bath . . ."

But these were the private achievements of his life ashore. He
continued active afloat, and in the year following the victory at

Preveza he successfully laid siege to the fortress of Castelnuovo which the Turkish army had failed to capture a few months previously. When the Spanish Governor, Don Francisco Sarmiento, finally surrendered, he and his remaining garrison were honorably and chivalrously treated. As the Abbé de Brantôme remarked of the expedition, "It was one of the greatest that he ever made against the Christians." In two years Barbarossa had shown himself superior to Doria at sea, and superior to his own Turkish army commanders in a military operation. It was no mean achievement for a man in his late fifties.

The outstanding event of the next few years was one in which Kheir-ed-Din personally took no part. Yet the whole action and the results stemming from it must be seen as owing themselves to the achievements of the two Barbarossa brothers. To avenge the defeat at Preveza, and to try to secure the western Mediterranean for his own navy and merchant marine, Charles V determined yet again to remove the threat of the Barbary corsairs—most of whom were men who had received their training under Kheir-ed-Din. The Kingdom of Algiers which the brothers had founded was proving an impossible irritant on the flank of Spain, and the raiders from North Africa had in no way declined in spirit since Barbarossa had left them in 1535. Under Barbarossa's successor, Hassan, the war against the Christian powers was prosecuted with a relentless venom. The Emperor decided that the only way to deal with the problem was to strike at its heart—Algiers. Though he had failed against the city in 1519, he would now have his revenge.

Throughout the winter of 1540 he had the dockyards of Spain and Naples busy with the preparation of an immense fleet, a fleet which would dwarf even the one with which Andrea Doria had so lamentably failed against Barbarossa. Unfortunately, the Emperor made the same mistake that had ruined the previous naval expedition—he sailed far too late in the year. It was not until

October that all the ships from Spain, from Genoa, from the papal dominions, and from Naples were assembled off Palma in Mallorca. The climate of adulation that surrounds kings and emperors is one which inevitably conditions them to believe that if they themselves are present nothing can go wrong with their plans. Despite the protests of Andrea Doria, the Emperor insisted that it was not too late to descend upon the city of Algiers and take it by storm.

On October 19 a fleet of over five hundred ships—already battered by a mistral—staggered into the Bay of Algiers. There were over one hundred Spanish sailing vessels laden with imperial troops from Germany and Italy; transports from Naples and Sicily; and all the chivalry of Spain embarked in two hundred galleons, escorted by fifty galleys. Among the Spanish gentlemen was Hernando Cortes, future conqueror of Mexico. It is estimated that about twenty-five thousand soldiers were embarked in the vast fleet that now prepared to invest Algiers.

Four days later the troops were all ashore. It looked as if Doria's gloomy prognostications about weather conditions off the Algerian coast were to be disproved. The sun shone, the sea was calm, and everything seemed set fair for a successful campaign. The local troops, Berbers and Moors, hurriedly withdrew before the overwhelming forces that were being landed. Almost without opposition the great invasion army began its march towards the city. To Hassan it must have seemed as if the end of his stewardship had come, and as if all that he had been entrusted with by Barbarossa would surely be lost to the Christians: just as the latter's brother, Aruj, had been lost in that lonely valley near Tlemcen twenty-three years ago.

Within a day of landing, the city was invested on all sides save the north. The cannon were being brought into position for the first onslaught, and the imperial troops and their master felt confident that at long last they would cut out the cancer of Algiers from North Africa. The first attack was scheduled for the morning of October 24, by which time the powder and shot and other stores and matériel should have been landed in sufficient quantities for the assault to begin. But on this occasion, unlike Doria at Preveza, the Emperor was not to be lucky with his weather. During the night of the 23rd, a typical autumn downpour developed. A cold front came sweeping down from the Mediterranean, to deluge the mountains behind the city and to turn the littoral into a morass of mud.

The morning of the 24th found the army harassed by gale-force winds and by cold driving rain. Powder got sodden, and the slow matches for the arquebuses and the cannon could scarcely be protected or kept alight. Far from this being the day when the great attack should have begun, the army now found itself in the unhappy role of being on the defensive.

Hassan and his Turks sallied out from the threatened city and put the attackers to flight. Demoralised by the weather, the Italian troops were the first to retire, soon to be followed by the Germans and the Spaniards. Only those indomitable warriors the Knights of Malta (who had provided a squadron of ships and a contingent of men for the expedition) refused to be stampeded by the attacking enemy. They chose, as always, the place of honour. If they had been attacking the city they would have been first into the breach, but now—since the army was retreating—it was they who formed the rear guard. As Lane-Poole wrote in *The Barbary Corsairs*: "The Knights of Malta, last of all, their scarlet doublets shining like a fresh wound, and their faces to the foe, covered the retreat."

Indeed, if that day of disaster for the Emperor proved anything, it was that fact—so well known in warfare—that it is not numbers that count, but discipline, training, and morale. Only the Knights of Malta seem to have emerged with credit from the bedraggled withdrawal of the imperial troops. Morgan tells in his

History of Algiers that "whenever any skirmish or action happened, and particularly in that notable encounter, talked of by the Turks to this very day, when the Cavaliers of Malta, gathering into a body, broke and defeated a strong party of Turks, and advanced so far as even to stick their daggers in the City Gate, called Beb-Azoun, it was Hassan Aga himself who, in person, repaired thither with the utmost diligence to remedy that disorder . . ."

Hassan at the head of his Turks now forced the knights to withdraw, but not to yield. Fighting all the way, they withstood the onslaught of Hassan's mounted troops and thus gave the army time to withdraw to its established positions; Charles V, his staff, and part of the troops taking up their station on a hillside overlooking the sea and the disembarkation point. Finally, late in that long, hard day, the Emperor and his cavalry came down in a body to help their gallant rear guard. Hassan's forces withdrew, but not before the Knights of Malta had lost a large part of their small force. "And to this day," as Morgan wrote, "the place where those valiant gentlemen bravely lost their lives, is usually pointed to by the Turks themselves, who call it the Cavaliers' Sepulchre, and largely commend their gallantry . . ."

The wind now reached gale force, and burst upon the anchored armada and the harsh Algerian shore. It veered from north to northeast, and the rolling breakers had the full fetch of the sea behind them, all the way from the Gulf of Genoa over six hundred miles away. The sailing galleons dragged as the raging winds seized upon their heavy top hamper, their lofty masts, and awkward yards. Some managed to claw their way offshore, but most of them were powerless to move. One after another they fell foul of their neighbours, or staggered with dragging anchors onto the rocks that fringed the foam-lashed beach. It was one of the worst maritime disasters in history. Throughout the night of the 25th and the morning of the following day, 140 sailing ships came to grief on the Algerian coast. So violent was the gale that for centuries afterwards it was referred to in Algiers as "Charles's Gale."

Hassan and his Turks, the native Berbers, and the expatriate Moors from Spain did not waste their opportunity. They fell upon the soldiers and sailors who staggered ashore and massacred them. "As the light increased, the scene appeared more horrible. The ships in the Bay had either broke their cables, or lost their anchorage, driving about at sea and dashing each other to pieces, or else running ashore and bilging on the rocks and strands. The same fate attended all the ships which had doubled the promontory of Apollo . . . The country Moors, beholding this destruction, swarmed to the seaside; and as the poor people were driving ashore, and in hopes of getting to the camp, they were piteously stripped naked and pierced through with lances by those merciless Africans, of both sexes, who were there waiting."

"Thy will be done"—these are reputedly the words of Charles V as he gazed down at his shattered fleet and ruined army. A retreat was ordered to the Bay of Matifou, some twenty miles east of Algiers, where the remnants of the fleet under Andrea Doria had managed to reassemble after the gale had blown itself out. Demoralised, lashed by blinding rain, the army was under constant attack from Hassan and his Turks, as well as all the local irregulars. Even when they had regained the ships their sufferings were not at an end, for a further northerly gale burst upon them. The fleet for a second time was scattered up and down the coast. When the Emperor and his ruined army and navy finally reached Spain at the end of November they had lost 8000 troops, 300 officers of the Spanish nobility, innumerable galleys, and 150 sailing ships. Spanish arms were not to suffer so great a disaster until the loss of the Armada sent against England by Charles V's son, Philip II. As Jurien de la Gravière drily

191

remarked: "The climate of Africa was clearly unsuited to deeds of chivalry."

One thing that the costly failure of Charles's expedition did establish for centuries to come was the security of the Kingdom of Algiers. Barbarossa's addition to the Ottoman power was destined to be a thorn in the side of all Europe until the nineteenth century. But whenever any thought of concerted action against the Barbary corsairs occurred to the rulers of Europe, there also returned the memory of that terrible disaster, when the God of Battles had shown himself on the side of the Moslems, and had "breathed and they were scattered." In Algiers itself the slave market was glutted, and in later years the Turks would often refer to 1541 as "the time when Christians sold at an onion per head."

20

HIGH ADMIRAL OF THE OTTOMANS

The last years of Barbarossa were marked, politically, by the conclusion of what has sometimes been called "the impious alliance" between France and the Sublime Porte. Francis I, that ruler so typical in many ways of Renaissance Man, was typical also in his cynicism when it came to politics. In his determination to counteract the ambitions of Charles V, he had early seen that the power of the new Turkish navy, which Kheir-ed-Din had created, had introduced a new factor upon the Mediterranean and, therefore, the European scene.

As early as 1536 a small combined force of Turkish and French ships had engaged in company against ships of the Spanish navy, and had subsequently wintered together in Marseilles. Although there is no documentary evidence to prove it, it seems more or less conclusive that at some time or other during this year a formal alliance between the two powers had been signed. If the aims of Francis I in aligning himself, at any rate at sea, with the Ottoman Empire are clear enough, it is hardly less difficult to comprehend the motives of that astute diplomat and ruler the Sultan Suleiman. His aim was the ultimate conquest of Europe, and if these Christians were divided one against another, then it was clearly to his advantage to make what use he could of their rivalries, enmities, and intrigues. As has been remarked before, the contempt in which the Moslem Turk held the European Christian was largely due to the patent evidence that these so-called lovers of the Prince of Peace were no more than self-seeking adventurers—less united, indeed, by their faith than were the nations of the Moslem world.

Although a number of French historians have recoiled from this alliance with the enemy of the Christian world, and although a number of historians of other European nations have enjoyed exposing the perfidy of France, there was little new in the situation. The French, for political, geographic, and economic reasons, have always been compelled to seek whatever alliances best suited their temporary convenience. They had not been slow to fall in with the plans of the Venetians in the thirteenth century to dismember the Christian Byzantine Empire for the mutual enrichment of France and Venice. They were not to be slow in later centuries to engage in treaties and agreements that may make the moralist raise his hands in pious despair. Curiously enough, the epithet "Perfidious Albion," conferred upon Great Britain by the French some centuries later, was perhaps not so much a mark of abuse as an unwilling compliment—the British had once or twice defeated the French at their own national game.

For Barbarossa, as for the Sultan, the alliance seemed to promise only advantage. He knew as well as his master that the real enemy of Turkey-in-Europe was the power of Spain and the Empire. Anything that served to hasten the dissolution of that complicated political and military machine could only be to the good of Turkey. He was well aware that the French navy was virtually negligible, and that it was only the coalition of Spain with Venice and Genoa which could in any way threaten Turkish supremacy in the Mediterranean. The obvious course of action, therefore, was to work with the French to the detriment of

Charles V. If ever the Emperor could be brought to the ground, there would then be little difficulty in disposing of France.

Sir Godfrey Fisher in *Barbary Legend* comments upon the political situation of the period: "As the rest of Christendom [at this time] appears to have lived in dread of the 'universal domination' of Spain, and the rift between France and Venice was so fundamental that they are said never to have fought side by side officially after 1504, it is not perhaps surprising that not only the inhabitants of Tunis but Catholics, Lutherans, and Greeks in Europe often preferred Turkish protection or rule, that oppressed Christians fled to the more free and enlightened atmosphere of Algiers, just as the Hungarians did to Turkish territory, and that even in distant England there was an element anxious to establish relations with the Sultans of Morocco and Turkey and with Kheir-ed-Din . . ."

It has to be remembered that the Moslem attitude towards other faiths and other nations was often more tolerant than that of the newly emergent European powers. The latter were so bedevilled by their militant nationalism that they could not comprehend how they might best work together to their common advantage. An almost identical situation to that of sixteenth-century Europe may be observed in parts of Africa and Asia in the second half of the twentieth century.

So, in 1543, at the pressing invitation of Francis I, the Sultan sent out his High Admiral with a fleet of one hundred galleys to assist the French against the Emperor. Clearly the aim of the expedition was to do as much harm to the Emperor's dominions as possible, and Barbarossa did not neglect any opportunities. Reggio, guarding the Strait of Messina from the north, was yet again sacked. According to one account, the Governor's daughter was captured and became Barbarossa's wife. "A most beautiful damsel," says Morgan, "of eighteen; with whom he became so enamoured that he married her, and in regard to his new spouse, released both her parents . . ."

The sun-baked coastline and villages of Calabria once more saw the advancing crescent of Turkish sails. The people fled inland to hill villages perched high above the azure sea, as the Turks, like fishermen dragging in a net, scooped up all the coastal traffic and all the men, women, and poor valuables of that impoverished land. Norman Douglas, recording in his *Old Calabria* the many tragedies that have befallen that part of southern Italy, remarks that though the portrait that has been painted of these Turkish raids is black enough, yet there were others even more culpable than the Moslems: "In Saracen times the Venetians actually sold Christian slaves to the Turks. Parrino cites the seven enactments which were issued in the sixteenth century against Christian sailors who decoyed children on board their boats and sold them as slaves to the Moslems. I question whether the Turks were ever guilty of a corresponding infamy." Describing the watchtowers which are so noticeable a feature of all this coast, he goes on to say: "The ominous name *Torre di Guardia* (tower of outlook)—a cliff whence the sea was scanned for the appearance of Turkish vessels—survives all over the south. Barbarossa, too, has left his mark; many a hill, fountain, or castle has been named after him . . ."

Passing north of Naples the fleet invested the castle that guarded the ancient city of Gaeta. Clearly this was more than a simple piratical raid—as some historians have described Kheired-Din's campaign of 1543. The raider or corsair does not attack fortified cities like Reggio, or deliberately lay siege to strong fortresses like that of Gaeta. It is quite clear that the Sultan's instructions to his High Admiral had been to inflict as much damage as possible upon the lands and dominions of the Emperor. Having captured the fortress and sacked the city, the fleet moved on northward for its rendezvous with the French forces in the Gulf of Lions at Marseilles.

That summer witnessed the surprising sight of a fleet belonging to the Sultan—a Moslem fleet, theoretically the enemy of all Christendom—passing peaceably along the Riviera coast of France. Once he had put the territory of Charles V behind him, Barbarossa saw to it that the conduct of his ships and sailors was impeccable. Of his later stay at Toulon one visitor to the city wrote, "To see Toulon one might imagine oneself at Constantinople, everyone pursuing his business with the greatest order and justice . . . Never did an army live in stricter or more orderly fashion than that one."

On arrival at Marseilles, Barbarossa was furious to find that none of the arrangements for which he had asked had been made. The French had failed to have the correct weight of provisions ready, the naval stores that had been requested had failed to arrive, and, in short, there was every evidence of dilatory incompetence. The man who had reorganised the dockyards of the Sultan, built the Turkish navy, and made it the most effective instrument in the Mediterranean was not used to such inefficiency. Received by the young Duke of Enghien, François de Bourbon, Barbarossa had no hesitation in telling him exactly what he thought of the arrangements—or, rather, the lack of them. He himself, observers noted with some surprise, was treated by the Duke and by all the nobility and senior French officers as a man of great consequence.

But despite the evidence of a number of chroniclers, the legend of the violent, piratical Old Man of the Sea dies hard. It is significant that it is mainly in French accounts that Barbarossa has acquired so unattractive a reputation. The reason for this is not too difficult to find. Barbarossa had been duped by the French and had been badly let down by them. Furthermore, it was the French themselves who later committed the atrocities which they then, and subsequently, found convenient to lay at the door of the Sultan's Admiral.

Having asked for the assistance of his Turkish ally, Francis I now found himself in the awkward position of being compelled to take action against Charles V. Yet he did not feel strong enough to engage the Emperor in a serious campaign, and he was also being roundly attacked in France for having allied himself with the Turks. It would have been bad enough, some reasoned, to conclude such an alliance (although possibly political advantageous). To have an immense Turkish fleet actually visiting the ports of France, thus openly proclaiming the alliance to all of Europe, was stupid and dangerous. It gave the enemies of France a good propaganda weapon against her, and it even inspired affection for the Emperor from people who otherwise resented his ambitions. Nevertheless, Francis had to produce some evidence that he was serious in his request for help, and that his troops were ready to take the field.

Barbarossa, after his disgust at French inefficiency in Marseilles, was probably prepared for what happened. The French King proposed an attack on Nice, to which the Turkish Admiral agreed. But the troops who were provided for the operation were no more efficient than the dockyard and commissariat of Marseilles, and when the combined Franco-Turkish fleet appeared off the city it was found that once again inefficiency reigned. Barbarossa is reputed to have exclaimed "What soldiers are these—that fill their vessels with wine casks and forget to bring their powder!" Even Montluc, the French Ambassador to Venice, was honest enough to admit in 1544 that during the Turkish expedition of the previous year the conduct, administration, and discipline of the Turkish forces had been far superior to that of any European powers. "They are more hardy," he wrote, "more obedient, and more enduring than us. They have one great advantage, that they think about nothing except war . . ." The Turks in fact were professionals—as they soon showed in the siege of Nice.

It was principally through the efficiency of the Turkish siege artillery that the city fell so quickly, a large breach having been opened in its walls. As was customary at the time, once the breach had been opened, the Governor of the besieged city or fortress was entitled to ask for honourable terms of surrender. Only if the besieged continued to resist until overwhelmed was a city deemed open to loot and slaughter. On this occasion the Governor formally surrendered his city, and the Franco-Turkish troops marched in. What happened next is not too difficult to disinter from the records that remain. It is important to do so, for the reason that later French libels accused the Turks of breaking faith and putting the city to fire and the sword. Nice, in any event, was sacked and burned to the ground. But who was responsible? Spanish accounts are unanimous that it was the French who burned the town, and having done so, then retreated to their base at Toulon. All the evidence goes to show that, at the time when Nice was sacked and burned, the Turkish fleet and gunners—their part in the operation already completed—had withdrawn to their anchorage at Villefranche. It was the French who had been left behind to garrison the town, for Barbarossa certainly had no interest in maintaining any troops there. In this connection Sir Godfrey Fisher quotes the evidence of the French Marshal Vieilleville: "The town of Nice was sacked in defiance of the capitulation terms, and it was then burned. But for this one must not blame Barbarossa and his troops, for they were already far off when this happened . . . This slander was put upon the unfortunate Barbarossa in order to uphold the honour and the reputation of France, indeed Christendom itself." Since there are sufficient tributes, both from French and Spanish sources, to the high quality of the discipline in Barbarossa's fleet and army, there can be no doubt where the truth of the matter lies.

Before withdrawing to his winter quarters of Toulon, Kheir-ed-Din despatched a squadron of galleys under Salah Rais to harry the Emperor's native Spain. They fell upon the unsuspecting coastline of Catalonia—for the Spaniards were under the impression that all Barbarossa's ships were in France—and sacked a number of ports and harbours. Salah Rais then withdrew to winter in Algiers, while Barbarossa and his fleet moved to Toulon. He had executed the Sultan's orders with his usual thoroughness. On both sides of the Mediterranean, in Italy and in Spain, he had inflicted considerable damage on Charles V's lands and peoples. He had done what was required of him by the French. He had shown all of Europe whose fleet it was that dominated the Mediterranean.

It is doubtful, however, whether the campaign had been of much real benefit to the Sultan, and certainly the French were not particularly reliable when it came to meeting their side of the bargain. In any case, within a year, the alliance was dead. Francis I, with yet another of his mercurial changes in foreign policy, had effected a pact with Charles V. By means of this both France and Spain were soon happily enabled to carve out considerable additions to their kingdoms from the northern Italian states. For the moment, though, the French and Turkish fleets rode out the winter side by side in Toulon harbour.

The alliance of Catholic French and Moslem Turk was curiously and obviously manifest to the French themselves, as well as to the rest of Europe, during those months. It is said, though on doubtful authority, that Barbarossa even forbade the French to have the church bells of Toulon rung to call the Christians to Mass. Certainly there was some incongruity in the spectacle of this great Moslem fleet, with its imams reciting the Koran to the faithful, at anchor in the main naval base of Catholic France. There was something incongruous, too, in the fact that aboard these vessels, and in the quarters set up for them ashore, the oarsmen were largely enslaved Italians, Spaniards, and even Frenchmen. The power of the Sultan and Barbarossa was never so manifest to Europe as in that winter of 1543.

In the spring of the following year, with the rations and pay of his fleet finally provided under the contract with Francis I, Kheir-ed-Din sailed for Constantinople. Despatches from the Sultan had no doubt advised him of the forthcoming *rapprochement* between Francis I and Charles V. In any case, even if he was not aware of this new shift in European alignments, the Sultan was unwilling to have the major part of his fleet absent from Constantinople for too long. The Knights of St. John were already beginning to show signs of increasing activity, now that they had established themselves in their new base in Malta. Individual pirates were still active in the Aegean, and there were many problems still unresolved in the islands of the archipelago.

On his passage back along the Riviera and through the Ligurian Sea, Barbarossa behaved with the absolute propriety of a visiting admiral on a fleet cruise. Indeed Ambassador Montluc again commented on the behavior of his fleet, and said that no other force, whether Moslem or Christian, had ever conducted itself so well. It was a different matter, of course, as soon as he came within reach of the territories of Charles V. The island of Elba, where so many years ago his brother Aruj had carried out that first successful attack on the papal galley, was ransacked. Moving on southward, right in the teeth of Charles's city of Naples, Kheir-ed-Din stormed the little island of Procida before turning upon fertile and gracious Ischia where he stored his ships with fruit, food, women, and men. The Lipari Islands, lying across the path of his advance southwards to Sicily, were also forced to pay their tribute of human beings and provisions.

In deference to his new wife and her parents, Reggio was left without any further depredation. The fleet turned eastward across the long acres of the soft Ionian and made its way to the Aegean. The High Admiral's homecoming was worthy of his achievements. From Santa Sophia and from all the great new mosques of Constantinople the lights shone out across the water as the people gathered in their thousands to witness the return of this man who had become a myth in his own lifetime. The straining oars beat up against the cold current of the Bosphorus as the ships rounded Seraglio Point and began to stream into the placid waters of the Horn. They had gold aboard and slaves, loot from Italy and Spain, money and gifts from France, and tribute from the Greek islands that had formerly belonged to Genoa and Venice. It was one of the greatest moments in the history of that fabulous harbour—a harbour which, in its time, had witnessed many triumphant scenes. The return of the King of the Sea to the Sublime Porte, to the capital of the giant Ottoman Empire, was one of the peaks in that empire's history. Eastern Europe lay humbled beneath the Sultan's armies, western Europe trembled at the threat of his approach, and east as far as Persia Turkish arms were supreme.

21

"THE KING OF THE SEA
IS DEAD"

In July 1546, within sight and sound of that fast-flowing current which had so often hurled his galleys southwards into the Aegean, Kheir-ed-Din Barbarossa died in his palace on the Bosphorus. Contrary to a later malicious French report that "he died exhausted by the manifold vices of the harem," Kheir-ed-Din was carried off by a fever—something that was not uncommon in midsummer Constantinople. He was sixty-three years old. He left only one known son, Hassan, the child of an Algerian woman, who was destined in his turn to become Pasha of Algiers and ruler of the Ottoman Kingdom of Algeria.

"Never even among the great Greek and Roman conquerors of lands and kingdoms," wrote the Abbé de Brantôme, "was there another such as he." This tribute coming from a Christian is all the more convincing since the Abbé was one of the greatest admirers of the Knights of St. John, Barbarossa's deadliest enemies. It may well have reflected the opinion of the knights themselves, for the Abbé spent some considerable time in Malta, even going out in the knights' galleys on their "caravans," or offensive sweeps against the Turks. "France or any other country," he added, "would have been proud to claim him as her son."

If his Christian contemporaries could find so much to admire in Kheir-ed-Din, it is hardly surprising that to the Turks he was, and remains, the epitome of the manly virtues. It was not only the fact that he was a great warrior—something which Turks have always respected—but he was also the first seaman of his time. Furthermore, by his industry, endurance, and patience he had founded a great kingdom that was to last for centuries.

There are few success stories equal to his. Born in a Greek island, the youngest son of an obscure Turkish soldier, he had risen by sheer force of character and endeavour to be the equal, and in many cases the superior, of kings and rulers who had been born to the purple. Morgan, quoting Haedo, remarks that his memory "is yet held in such veneration among the Turks, particularly the seafaring people, that no voyage is undertaken from Constantinople, by either public or private persons, without their first visiting his tomb, whereat they say a *Fedha,* or formulary sort of prayer for success, being the first chapter of the Koran; saluting the remains of so efficacious an individual with repeated vollies of great and small fire-arms, both at their arrival and departure. All of which is done with much ceremony and singular solemnity . . ."

In 1551, five years after his death, his great lieutenant, Torghoud, or Dragut as he was known in Europe, managed to wrest the fortress of Tripoli away from the Knights of St. John, thus posing yet a further threat to Spanish communications with Sicily and the Levant. Dragut, who was as formidable at sea as Barbarossa—he has been described as "a living chart of the Mediterranean"—became Sultan of Tripoli, where his tomb can still be seen. In 1565, aged eighty, he was killed during the siege of Malta. But prior to this, he had achieved another major success for Turkish arms. In 1560 in company with Piali, Barbarossa's successor as Admiral of the Fleet, he had inflicted a crushing defeat upon the Spanish navy in the vicinity of Barbarossa's old hideout, the island of Djerba. Philip II had by now succeeded his father, Charles V, to the throne of Spain, and it was said that the two greatest defeats he suffered in his lifetime were the Armada against England and the battle off Djerba against the Turks.

In the years that were to follow, the stability of Turkish Algeria was even further ensured by Hassan, the son of Barbarossa. He drove the Spaniards out of all but their last remaining position of importance in North Africa, the city of Oran. A few years later another great Turkish sea captain, Ochiali, was harrying the coast of Spain and making active preparations for the reconquest of Tunis. Tunis together with its Spanish fortress of La Goletta finally fell to the Turks in 1574.

The great setback to Ottoman sea power during the years following Kheir-ed-Din's death was of course the defeat at Lepanto in 1571. It is worth remarking that the only section of the navy which distinguished itself in this battle was the Algerian squadron under the command of Ochiali. Lepanto, that last great sea battle in which the oared galley predominated, was a triumph for the European powers. Yet, curiously enough, within a very few years the over-all picture of sea power in the Mediterranean was hardly any different from that which had existed at the peak of Kheir-ed-Din's career. With nearly the whole of the North African coast, including both Tunis and Algiers, in Turkish hands, the galleys, galleots, and the new sailing galleons of the Ottoman Empire in the West were able to roam almost unchallenged from the Atlantic to the Levant.

The two great events which shook Turkish sea power during these years were the failure of Turkish arms at the siege of Malta in 1565, and the decisive defeat of the fleet at Lepanto six years later. But both these failures proved in the end to have relatively little effect upon the Ottoman dominance of the inland sea.

It was not until the nineteenth century that American and British successes in Tripoli and Algiers paved the way for the subjugation of North Africa by the French. It was, indeed, the French who administered the *coup de grâce* on July 5, 1830, when the last Mohammedan ruler of Algiers sailed in exile for Naples. Norman Douglas is correct, however, when he remarks in *Old Calabria:* "It is all very well for Admiral de la Gravière to speak of 'Gallia Victrix'—the Americans, too, might have something to say upon that point. The fact is that neither European nor American arms crushed the pest. But for the invention of steam, the Barbary corsairs might still be with us."

French rule in North Africa has proved to be only temporary. Today, once again, a succession of Mohammedan kingdoms stretches from Egypt in the east to Morocco in the west. The shadow of Kheir-ed-Din, "the Protector of Religion," has never left these shores. He lived in the last great age of the galleys, the vessel that had dominated naval warfare in the Mediterranean since the days of the Carthaginians. He lived to see the age when heavy cannon mounted aboard large sailing vessels rendered the galley obsolete. The battle of Preveza, where the distinguished Venetian Alessandro Condalmiero showed how to manage a galleon in action, foreshadowed the end of the galley. Nevertheless, galleys continued to be used by navies in the Mediterranean well into the nineteenth century.

Barbarossa, although his greatness was recognised by French, Spanish, and even English chroniclers during his lifetime, was to be traduced in the centuries that were to follow. The French were prominent among those who did their best to discredit him, being uneasy and ashamed for that period in their history when they had concluded their alliance with the enemy of Christian Europe. In other countries historians tended to reduce him to no more than a footnote. The eyes of Europeans were turned more and more towards the Atlantic and the new oceanic trade routes with the East. What happened in the Mediterranean in the sixteenth century seemed to them relatively unimportant compared to what was happening in the Caribbean or the Pacific.

The Turks have never forgotten their debt to him. In the new kingdoms of North Africa his name is still held in the same reverence as is that of Nelson in England, or John Paul Jones in America. In Turkey he is the subject of many children's books, and he often appears in cartoon magazines where he features as a cross between a Turkish Francis Drake and Robin Hood. His eternal appeal lies not only in his achievements, but in the fact that he is one of the most outstanding examples of "poor boy makes good." For thousands of the underfed and underprivileged in Moslem countries he still holds out the example of hope. His life was violent, his death peaceful, and his achievements extraordinary. The Turkish annals for the year 1546 record simply: "The King of the Sea is dead."

BIBLIOGRAPHY

Anderson, R. C., *Oared Fighting Ships*, 1962

Bergerac, J. M. de, *Memoirs d'un Protestant Condamné aux Galères*, 1757

Brantôme, L'Abbé de, *Vie des Hommes Illustres et Grands Capitaines Étrangers de son Temps*, 1822

Broadley, A. M., *Tunis, Past and Present*, 1882

Chenier, L. S., *Cruelties of the Algerian Pirates*, 1816

———, *Present State of the Empire of Morocco*, 1788

Currey, E. H., *Sea-Wolves of the Mediterranean*, 1910

Dan, Père F., *Histoire de Barbarie et de ses Corsaires*, 1649

Edrisi, El, *Description de l'Afrique et de l'Espagne*, 1866

Fisher, Sir G., *Barbary Legend*, 1957

Furttenbach, J., *Architectura Navalis*, 1629

Grammont, H. de, *Histoire d'Alger*, 1887

Gravière, Admiral J. de la, *Les Derniers Jours de la Marine à Rames*, 1885

———, *Doria et Barberousse*, 1886

———, *Les Corsaires Barbaresques*, 1887

BIBLIOGRAPHY

Haedo, D. de, *Topographia e Historia General de Argel,* 1612

Hajji Khalifa, *History of the Maritime Wars of the Turks,* Translated 1831

Hammer, J. von, *History of the Ottoman Empire,* 1836

La Roerie, G., and Vivielle, J., *Navires et Marins de la Rame à l'Helice,* 1930

Lane, F. C., *Venetian Ships and Shipbuilders of the Renaissance,* 1934

Lane-Poole, S., *The Story of the Barbary Corsairs,* 1890

Marmol, L., *Descripcion de Africa,* 1573

Morgan, J., *A Complete History of Algiers,* 1731

Newman, P. H., *Ancient Sea Galleys,* 1915

Pantera, Pantero, *L'Armata Navale,* 1614

Rashid, Ekrem, *La Vie de Khaireddine Barberousse,* 1931

Rousseau, Baron A., *History of the Conquest of Tunis by the Ottomans,* 1883

Sandoval, Bishop P. de, *Historia de Carlos Quinto,* 1614

Taylor, E. G. R., *The Haven-Finding Art,* 1957

Torr, C., *Ancient Ships,* 1894

Vertot, L'Abbé de, *Histoire des Chevaliers de Malte,* 1726

NOTES

I am indebted to the London Library for a number of the books consulted, also to the authorities of the Royal Malta Library for all their assistance over many months. Extensive use has been made of J. Morgan's *A Complete History of Algiers* (1731). Morgan's work, while discursive and amusing, is quite often unreliable. The quotations from it, accordingly, have been taken as far as possible from sections where facts can be checked against other authorities.

Since Morgan's somewhat baroque prose seems to me to catch the flavour of the times I have also used a number of his translations from the Abbot Diego de Haedo. The latter is by far the most trustworthy authority on matters relating to Kheir-ed-Din. He lived in Algiers for many years not long after the latter's death, and knew many of his friends, fellow seamen, and servants. Hajji Khalifa, who in the seventeenth century wrote a *History of the Maritime Wars of the Turks,* is more reliable when it comes to details of Kheir-ed-Din's life in Constantinople and the formation of the Ottoman Navy. For general background information and for matters of Turkish policy I am largely indebted to J. von Hammer's monumental *History of the Ottoman Empire* (1836). In the notes to each chapter I have indicated in order the principal authorities from whom quotations have been made.

CHAPTER 1

J. Morgan, *A Complete History of Algiers*, 1731.

H. R. P. Dickson, *The Arab of the Desert*, 1949.

J. E. Flecker, *Hassan*, 1922.

For details of life aboard the galleys I have drawn largely upon the work of Pantero Pantera, *L'Armata Navale* (1614), also on the eighteenth-century memoirs of J. M. de Bergerac, who was condemned to serve in the French galleys for being a Protestant. J. Furttenbach's *Architectura Navalis* (1629) and the works of Admiral J. de la Gravière have provided many details of construction and management.

CHAPTER 2

Sir G. Fisher, *Barbary Legend*, 1957.

S. Lane-Poole, *Barbary Corsairs*, 1890.

J. Morgan, *op. cit.*

CHAPTER 3

J. Morgan, *op. cit.*

E. H. Currey, *Sea-Wolves of the Mediterranean*, 1910.

Throughout this chapter and elsewhere, in discussing meteorology, sea and coastal conditions, etc., I have made considerable use of the invaluable section in the *Admiralty Pilot for the Mediterranean*, Vol. III, 1957, dealing with weather and local phenomena, as well as drawing upon personal experience from a number of years spent sailing in these waters.

CHAPTER 4

J. Morgan, *op. cit.*

CHAPTER 5

J. Morgan, *op. cit.*

Diego de Haedo, *Topographia e Historia General de Argel,* 1612.

CHAPTER 6

J. Morgan, *op. cit.*
Diego de Haedo, *op. cit.*

CHAPTER 7

J. Morgan, *op. cit.*
J. E. Flecker, *op. cit.*
Sir G. Fisher, *op. cit.*

CHAPTER 8

J. Morgan, *op. cit.*
Sir G. Fisher, *op. cit.*
E. H. Currey, *op. cit.*

CHAPTER 9

J. Morgan, *op. cit.*

The quotation relating to the suitability of different races for work in the galleys is taken from *Navires et Marins de la Rame à l'Helice* by G. La Roerie and J. Vivielle (1930), a book which contains a considerable amount of valuable information on early vessels.

CHAPTER 10

S. Lane-Poole, *op. cit.*

J. Morgan, *op. cit.*

J. M. de Bergerac, *Memoirs d'un Protestant Condamné aux Galères,* 1757.

Rudyard Kipling, "The Finest Story in the World" from *Many Inventions,* 1893.

CHAPTER 11

J. Morgan, *op. cit.*

S. Lane-Poole, *op. cit.*

Sir G. Fisher, *op. cit.*

E. H. Currey, *op. cit.*

Bishop Sandoval of Pamplona, who wrote a *History of Charles V* (1614), is here, and elsewhere, an excellent corrective to some other authorities. He gives a very fair picture of the activities of Kheir-ed-Din and others during this period.

CHAPTER 12

S. Lane-Poole, *op. cit.*

I have also drawn extensively throughout this chapter on Professor E. G. R. Taylor's *The Haven-Finding Art* (1957), that outstanding history of marine navigational methods throughout the centuries. With regard to the use of dead reckoning in the Mediterranean, I spent some three years sailing a small yacht in most of the areas dealt with in this book without making any use of sextant or other aids except a compass and half a dozen charts. Even allowing for the fact that these modern charts were completely accurate, it proved to my own satisfaction that, provided a log is efficiently kept, it is possible to make accurate landfalls in this tideless sea with very simple methods and instruments.

CHAPTER 14

S. Lane-Poole, *op. cit.*

J. Morgan, *op. cit.*

CHAPTER 15

Sir G. Fisher, *op. cit.*

CHAPTER 17

E. H. Currey, *op. cit.*

CHAPTER 19

J. Morgan, *op. cit.*

CHAPTER 20

Sir G. Fisher, *op. cit.*

CHAPTER 21

Kheir-ed-Din's tomb is at Beshiktash, on the Pera side of the Golden Horn. When in Istanbul, I was interested to see how many "pulp" magazines and monthly strip-cartoon publications featured Kheir-ed-Din Barbarossa. Over four centuries after his death he is still very much remembered in the old capital of Turkey.

INDEX

217

THE MEDITERRANEAN

0   100   200   300   Miles